3-MINUTE
DEVOTIONS TO
LAUGH AND
REFLECT

3-MINUTE DEVOTIONS TO LAUGH AND REFLECT

LIGHTEN YOUR LOAD AND BRIGHTEN YOUR DAY

CHRISTOPHER D. HUDSON, AND STAN CAMPBELL

ILLUSTRATIONS BY DENNIS FLETCHER

BETHANYHOUSE

a division of Baker Publishing Group
Minneapolis, Minnesota

© 2021 by Christopher Hudson & Associates, Inc.

Published by Bethany House Publishers
11400 Hampshire Avenue South
Minneapolis, Minnesota 55438
www.bethanyhouse.com

Bethany House Publishers is a division of
Baker Publishing Group, Grand Rapids, Michigan

Printed in the United States of America

Library of Congress Cataloging-in-Publication Data
Names: Hudson, Christopher D., author. | Campbell, Stan, author.
Title: 3-minute devotions to laugh and reflect : lighten your load and brighten your day / Christopher D. Hudson, Stan Campbell.
Description: Minneapolis, Minnesota : Bethany House, a division of Baker Publishing Group, [2021]
Identifiers: LCCN 2021028778 | ISBN 9780764239687 (casebound) | ISBN 9780764234415 (paperback) | ISBN 9781493433537 (ebook)
Subjects: LCSH: Joy—Religious aspects—Christianity—Meditations. | Laughter—Religious aspects—Christianity—Meditations. | Christian life—Meditations.
Classification: LCC BV4647.J68 H83 2021 | DDC 248.4—dc23
LC record available at https://lccn.loc.gov/2021028778

Unless otherwise indicated, Scripture quotations are from THE HOLY BIBLE, NEW INTER-NATIONAL VERSION®, NIV® Copyright © 1973, 1978, 1984, 2011 by Biblica, Inc.® Used by permission. All rights reserved worldwide.

Scripture quotations marked MESSAGE are taken from THE MESSAGE, copyright © 1993, 2002, 2018 by Eugene H. Peterson. Used by permission of NavPress. All rights reserved. Represented by Tyndale House Publishers, Inc.

Cover design by Rob Williams, InsideOut Creative Arts, Inc.
Front cover and interior cartoons © Dennis Fletcher. Used by permission.

Authors represented by The Steve Laube Agency

22 23 24 25 26 27   7 6 5 4 3 2

Contents

Contents

3-MINUTE DEVOTIONS TO LAUGH AND REFLECT

". . . A bit of highlighting in Matthew,
but Leviticus, Numbers, Deuteronomy,
and Obadiah are like new."

Start to Finish

> All Scripture is God-breathed and is useful for teaching, rebuking, correcting and training in righteousness.
>
> 2 Timothy 3:16

Imagine receiving a new cookbook, flipping through it, and then choosing one ingredient from the appetizer section, one from salads, one from desserts, and so forth, to combine as you prepare a meal. Selecting your ingredients in this way will likely result in a meal resembling chocolate asparagus tuna burritos.

While it's a ridiculous idea, many of us read the Bible with that kind of random approach. It's natural to have our favorite passages. Many people are fond of the honest and descriptive poetry of the Psalms. Some focus on the teachings and parables of Jesus. Some like the Old Testament action stories. Others are intrigued by the apostle Paul's doctrinal truths and logic. And some people repeatedly return to Revelation to generate spirited discussions as they speculate about end times.

We must remember, however, that the Bible is a unified story. All that diversity of style and content is part of *the same* story. It's fine to read the sections we know and love, yet we must also fill in the blanks to discover the full truth revealed in Scripture. Those infrequently read portions might cast fresh light on your favorite passages. And you'll discover that when all the ingredients blend in proper proportions, the result will be delicious.

"I never make a decision without seeking wise counsel . . .
My last Internet search lasted three hours."

Help Wanted

Plans fail for lack of counsel, but with many advisers they succeed.

Proverbs 15:22

Did you ever play Gossip? In this game you sit in a circle of people, one person begins by whispering something into the ear of the person on his or her right, and the message is relayed from person to person until it gets back to the originator. Along the way, no one can repeat what they said or question what was said. Each person must simply pass along whatever he or she heard. Usually the ending statement is nothing like the original message.

We live in a wonderful time when we can carry the entire internet on a handheld device. If you get lost, clear directions pop up to help. Answers to most problems can be pulled up in milliseconds. Unfortunately, the internet has become an electronic version of Gossip: What you read may have been repeated and distorted so many times that it is no longer accurate.

Bad advice can be dangerous. When you have a serious problem—or when you are really, truly lost—why seek answers from an electronic or disinterested source? Instead, look around and find someone who has had a similar problem, someone who can provide trustworthy guidance. When God speaks through people who offer personal experience combined with personal concern for you, you won't need other advice.

"I like the preaching,
but the people seem a bit cold."

What's Your Spiritual Temperature?

I know your deeds, that you are neither cold nor hot. I wish you were either one or the other!

Revelation 3:15

You go to your doctor for a checkup and your temperature is 98.6 degrees. Average. You're both happy.

Some of us shoot for average spiritual temperature as well. We resist becoming so extreme that people accuse us of being religious fanatics, yet we don't want to be perceived as spiritual slackers either. It's like we set an internal "spiritual thermostat" to keep from being too hot or too cold in comparison to others.

But when it comes to spiritual temperature, "average" is nothing to be happy about. Jesus told the believers in the Laodicean church (through the apostle John): "Because you are lukewarm—neither hot nor cold—I am about to spit you out of my mouth" (Revelation 3:16). Jesus wants nothing to do with tepid faith.

When our love for God begins to run cold, we become prodigal children, lost sheep, lights unseen beneath a basket. If we realize what we're missing, we are eager to reconnect with him. But as long as we hover in an "average" comfort zone, we are like the Laodiceans—active for God but simply going through the motions.

The best option is to "run hot" for God. In our relationship with him, running a fever is a sign of excellent health.

"To establish rapport with our neighbors,
I'm participating in today's
'Ban Church Bells Before Noon'
demonstration."

Play Nice

If it is possible, as far as it depends on you, live at peace with everyone.

Romans 12:18

The tension between the church and the world has existed for centuries. Believers are instructed to share the love of Christ with others *and* to be careful not to get caught up in worldly things. Attempting to follow both commands simultaneously can be tricky and stress inducing.

On one hand, it can be tempting to withdraw from secular culture as we seek to avoid any threat of sin or compromise. But if we do so, how can we influence others for the kingdom? On the other hand, we can become so eager to connect with others that we ignore important church doctrines and traditions, even watering down potentially divisive aspects of the message of salvation.

Is it possible to comply with both scriptural commands? Peter offered sound advice to believers in the first century that we should follow in the twenty-first century: "Live such good lives among the pagans that, though they accuse you of doing wrong, they may see your good deeds and glorify God" (1 Peter 2:12).

We teach our kids to "play nice" with others who look, behave, and believe differently. Can't we do the same without sacrificing our own beliefs? After all, people are watching. Your behavior may be the first (or only) perception they have of the Gospel.

"The question isn't, 'Is it effective?'
The question is, 'Is it biblical?'"

Behaving outside the Box

If one part [of the body] suffers, every part suffers with it.
1 Corinthians 12:26

When a hockey player is charged with an infraction, he is sent to the penalty box for a specific period of time. His team is forced to play one person short, giving the opponent a significant advantage.

A similar penalty system works among believers within the church. Whenever one person is sidelined for any reason, the whole team suffers. Some things can't be helped; we all withdraw occasionally to deal with personal tragedies, crises of faith, and other unavoidable aspects of life. Too often, however, needless "time-outs" are entirely self-inflicted due to disobedience, improper involvements, laziness, and so forth. Some of us believe such spiritual indiscretions are victimless crimes, but that is not the case.

God has given different gifts, callings, and responsibilities to every member of his body, the church. Each person's contribution is essential for the good of the team. When you're not in play, the rest of us are not as effective as we could be.

Don't leave your team shorthanded as you watch from the sidelines. Do whatever it takes to stay out of the penalty box and remain involved. The rest of us need you.

"Our challenge is to take the Seniors' Ministry
to the next level . . .
<u>without</u> involving stairs."

Aging Grace, How Sweet the Sound

I'm just as vigorous to go out to battle now as I was then.
Joshua 14:11

Much has been written about respecting your elders. What is less frequently emphasized, however, is respecting yourself as you age. As people retire from (or are pushed out of) productive jobs, too many seem to retire from spiritual commitment as well.

Why is this the case? Spiritual warfare can at times be demanding, if not exhausting. Consistently holding to one's faith during hard times is a challenge at any age, but especially when physical health begins to decline and mental acuity starts to slip a bit.

Not many of us have the mentality (or stamina) of Caleb, who at eighty-five was just as eager to do battle as he had been at forty. Not many people would be up to such a challenge. More frequently, however, God revises callings of his people to suit their age. In his wonderful grace, he provides gifts and opportunities for aging people that they didn't have as youngsters: accumulated wisdom to share, increased empathy for the pains and fears of others, willingness to listen to and mentor others, ample time for service, and more.

Stop dwelling so much on what you were once able to do, and see what you need to be doing today. You may not be on the front lines any longer, but you're still in the fight!

"To save money, we're turning lights off in unused rooms . . .
If you'll get the Fasting Chapel,
I'll get the Cell Phone Free Youth Hall."

Easy Won't Do It

Physical training is of some value, but godliness has value for all things, holding promise for both the present life and the life to come.

1 Timothy 4:8

"Try this. It's good for you."

How do you respond to this appeal from a friend or associate? Many people are reluctant, skeptical, or wary. We've learned through previous experience that while something may indeed be good for us, it's not at all pleasant!

Besides, we already know what's good for us, don't we? We write New Year's resolutions, we go on diets, and we join gyms. But then we break the resolutions by January 15, forget the diet at the first sign of dessert, and speak proudly of our gym membership while never actually working out there.

Most things that are truly good for us require discipline, which is rarely easy or fun. Spiritual disciplines are particularly worthwhile, but they require more than a casual, intermittent effort. Quieting oneself before God for prayer and meditation, fasting, sacrificial giving, confession, and other disciplines requires determination. These "spiritual workouts" will help us draw closer to and become more like our Lord.

If you've become skittish about self-improvement recommendations, consider a new regimen of spiritual discipline. It may not be easy at first, but it will eventually become enjoyable—and it's definitely good for you!

An experienced pastor can usually spot
those who have issues with authority.

Feed Your Ox

> The elders who direct the affairs of the church well are worthy of double honor, especially those whose work is preaching and teaching.
>
> 1 Timothy 5:17

While the average churchgoer has an idea of what a pastor's life is like, that image probably falls far short of reality. Most pastors are on call all the time. It's an unrelenting job, and often a thankless one.

Do you want to know the meaning of life or why bad things happen to good people? Ask the pastor to explain in twenty-five words or less. What if one church business owner won't give a fellow churchgoer a 50 percent discount? Schedule a pastoral appointment for mediation (and anger management). Is the church kitchen out of coffee? Call the pastor; wake him up if necessary.

Amid weddings, baptisms, funerals, sermons, Bible studies, confirmation classes, visitations, and endless church activities, pastors hear a lot of complaints. Does yours ever hear a compliment?

First Timothy 5:17 is based on an Old Testament command: "Do not muzzle an ox while it is treading out the grain" (Deuteronomy 25:4; 1 Timothy 5:18). In other words, don't ignore the needs of the one who is doing the work.

The second Sunday in October has been designated as Pastor Appreciation Day. But surely your pastor deserves your gratitude throughout the year, tangibly expressed through occasional hugs or handshakes, meaningful cards, invitations to dinner, or similar actions. Wouldn't today be a great day to start?

"We need some variety in our prayer life . . .
Tonight, <u>I'll</u> pray for peace and wisdom,
and <u>you</u> can pray for the new bass boat."

Not the Response You Were Looking For?

I was given a thorn in my flesh. . . . Three times I pleaded with the Lord to take it away from me.

2 Corinthians 12:7–8

We may boldly affirm that our omnipotent, loving, giving God promises to meet all our needs. Sometimes, however, we are befuddled when God says no to one of our requests.

You'd think that if anyone deserved an affirmative response to his prayer requests, it would be the apostle Paul. He suffered and sacrificed for God every day. Yet God turned down Paul's passionate (and seemingly reasonable) plea to remove a serious physical impediment, which Paul described as "a messenger of Satan, to torment" him.

Why did God say no? He explained, "My grace is sufficient for you, for my power is made perfect in weakness" (2 Corinthians 12:9). Paul's need for grace from God was greater than his need to get rid of his "thorn." God declined Paul's request so Paul could become stronger. Paul learned, as we should, that human limitations and trying times can allow us to experience Christ's strength to a greater degree.

We don't always understand why God says no to our requests. Yet even when we don't, we can be confident he always has a good reason.

"The church time capsule contained a Flannel-graph,
a list of members from 1918,
and the same hymnal we used last Sunday."

Tradition vs. Change

He who is the Glory of Israel does not lie or change his mind;
for he is not a human being, that he should change his mind.

1 Samuel 15:29

God never changes. Being omnipotent, omniscient, and perfect, he has no need. But people do change, along with situations, cultures, and even churches. Not surprisingly, conflict and confusion can arise as some people cling to meaningful "godly" traditions while others want to adopt newer worship practices, outreach methods, or music styles.

In an attempt to be more culturally "relevant," some churches replace hymnals with on-screen lyrics, remodel church foyers into coffee bars, relocate stained-glass windows to a prayer chapel so they can brighten up the revamped sanctuary, and store the organ to make room for a rockin' praise band. While some members delight in such changes, others see them as spiritual travesties.

With the plethora of churches in many areas, we can shop around until we find exactly what we want. Or we can stay put, dig in our heels, and loudly bewail every little change. Meanwhile, God reminds his church that we are to be one body. If we can't agree on music styles or carpet colors, how can we unite on larger issues?

We would do well to follow the guidelines of Rupertus Meldenius, a seventeenth-century German Lutheran theologian who said, "In essentials unity, in non-essentials liberty, in all things charity."

"Rats!
The sermon is about the dangers of success! . . .
I was hoping for something you could apply to your life!"

Measures of Success

What does the LORD require of you? To act justly and to love
mercy and to walk humbly with your God.

Micah 6:8

How do you determine if someone is a success? Is it a financial measure: the car he drives, the clothes she wears, the large home they
decorate so elaborately? Is it a matter of relationships: a strong mar-
riage, a family whose members appear to avoid internal hostility, a
popular social media post? Is it an emotional accomplishment: a care-
free spirit, a perpetual smile, a mysterious sense of satisfaction with
life? What standards do you use to evaluate the successes of others?

Another question is harder to answer: How do you determine if *you*
are a success? If you use any of the previous standards, you'll almost
always find someone wealthier, happier, and more composed than you
are. Does that make you a failure?

Success is relative. It comes only if you accomplish what *you* are
aiming for. Rather than comparing ourselves to others, it's a lot less
stressful to shoot for God's standards of mercy and humility. They are
much more achievable than luxurious wealth and widespread popularity. Even better, when we use God's standards, he determines our level
of success, not us (Matthew 25:34–40).

Act justly. Love mercy. Walk humbly with your God. Success is that
simple—and that hard.

"I'm the official Greeter this morning . . .
Any unauthorized expressions of hospitality
do not necessarily reflect the beliefs,
by-laws, or demographics of this congregation."

Back Off!

It is true that some preach Christ out of envy and rivalry.
Philippians 1:15

Anyone with much church experience has probably encountered someone who is overprotective about his or her area of ministry. Deacon Jones is in charge of the church van—he holds the only key so no one can take it without his permission. Mrs. Smith has overseen the church kitchen since the Reagan administration; she gets hysterical every time someone leaves a spoon out of place. And assistant pastor Conway lives for those Sundays when the senior pastor is sick or out of town so he can give the congregation a "real" sermon.

Competition within the church is regrettable, but it's often wide-spread. This has been true for centuries. Paul's critics celebrated when he was in prison: "We're preaching and you're not!" Even so, Paul was wise enough to know that even though those guys "preach[ed] Christ out of selfish ambition," God's Word was being shared with people who needed to hear it. Meanwhile, Paul directed his ministry to the soldiers, prisoners, and visitors around him in prison (Philippians 1:12–14).

If you bump into an overzealous servant of God who is off-putting (which is likely to happen), don't let it bother you. Smile outwardly, laugh to yourself, thank God for his work that is being done, and carry on in your own service to the kingdom.

A secular business would just let her go.

Empowering or Enabling?

Carry each other's burdens, and in this way you will fulfill the law of Christ.

Galatians 6:2

The church is (and should be) a magnet for people who can't find what they're looking for in the secular world. For many, it is a place where they receive encouragement and support from fellow believers, discover and use their spiritual gifts, and find a calling that brings purpose and fulfillment to life.

Occasionally, however, some people think the church is there only for their benefit. They discover an abundance of love and grace, but rather than becoming motivated by it, they expect others to cater to them in their laziness and lack of commitment.

The church is not a day care center for adults who refuse to mature. It's not a resort where slackers can loiter, expecting other "servants" to provide them with whatever they need. Instead, the church is a place to become empowered, not enabled. Yes, Paul urged believers to "carry each other's burdens," but he immediately added the expectation for each person to "carry their own load" (Galatians 6:5).

So come to church when you're hurting and find the healing and peace we all crave. But then, when you're back on your feet, look around to find someone *you* can help. We're all on the same journey, and we're all expected to attend to one another. Join the race, find your pace, and carry on in God's strength and grace.

"I'm not a 'visual' learner . . .
so there may be extended periods
when my eyes will be closed."

Hard of Hearing?

Whoever has ears, let them hear.
Matthew 11:15

Jesus repeatedly reminded his followers that because God had given them ears, they ought to use them. God speaks clearly, in various ways, yet we too often miss what he is trying to tell us. We daydream through Bible studies, quiet times, and church committee meetings. We nod off during sermons. We stream music while we pray and end up listening to the music more than we listen to the Lord.

God can get anyone's attention whenever he wants to. In Scripture he used talking donkeys, burning bushes, wet-one-day-dry-the-next fleeces, quiet whispers, and other methods to draw a distressed or distracted person's attention to what he was saying or doing. Those are extraordinary examples, of course. Most often, God speaks clearly and consistently through his written Word, the Bible, which requires us to quiet our lives so we can hear it.

It's been noted that if you rearrange the letters in the word *listen*, you get *silent*. Silence, however, is only an initial step. Listening is then an intentional action that connects you to another person. It's not good when a failure to listen causes us to miss the needs and concerns of those around us. But if we miss what God is saying to us, we will really regret it.

You have ears. Silence the noise around you, and then put your ears to use!

"Before we commit to any high risk,
high reward expressions of faith,
let's see if the coffee's any good."

Enticements

Let us then approach God's throne of grace with confidence, so that we may receive mercy and find grace to help us in our time of need.

Hebrews 4:16

When people commit to going on a diet or starting an exercise regimen, it usually doesn't take long for the discipline to become routine and unpleasant. In short time, they may (consciously or unconsciously) create a reward system: perhaps a cheat meal or a day off. Often, however, the rewards increase until all commitment has diminished.

What is your incentive to strengthen your faith? What do you do when church attendance, prayer commitments, and daily quiet times with God become mundane or even boring? Adam and Eve ate forbidden fruit in an attempt to "be like God" (Genesis 3:5). The Israelites built a golden calf to enhance their spiritual enthusiasm (Exodus 32). We probably all know the results of those enticements.

Let's not make the same mistake. The almighty Lord of the universe has forgiven us and invites us to stand boldly before his throne to receive whatever help we need. What other possible motivation could we need?

All of us will go through periods when spiritual discipline seems routine and unproductive. But the answer isn't to turn elsewhere; it's to draw closer to God.

"... Three ... four ... five ... six ...
Looks like a unanimous vote
for a coffee bar in the church foyer."

Needy or Just Greedy?

My God will meet all your needs according to the riches of his glory in Christ Jesus.

Philippians 4:19

"I need a drink!"

"I can't start the day until I've had my morning latte."

"Now that I have a new Lexus, I just couldn't live without it."

It's amazing how quickly people can redefine their wants as needs. Truthfully, anyone's list of genuine needs is remarkably short. One such list included nine fundamental human needs: subsistence, protection, affection, understanding, participation, leisure, creation, identity, and freedom.[1]

Nowhere on that list do we find alcohol, coffee, or a new automobile. So when we read that God will meet all our needs yet find ourselves caffeine deprived and at wits' end one morning, do we unleash our frustration on him? When we can't afford a new vehicle every year or so, do we accuse God of failing to follow through on his promises?

Or have we discovered that what we most need from God is his ongoing love, forgiveness, mercy, and grace? When we have salvation, eternal life, and abundant blessings we don't deserve, it's rather insulting to God when we complain about material things we must "suffer" without.

Wants and needs are different. The sooner we learn the difference, the sooner we can experience the joy of being content with what God graciously provides for us.

"Each evening, I talk over the events of the day with God . . .
Your apology would drastically shorten tonight's session."

No Spiritual Bypasses

Leave your gift there in front of the altar. First go and be reconciled to [your brother or sister].

Matthew 5:24

The United States Interstate Highway System is designed to maximize efficiency and ease of travel for drivers going long distances (though you might dispute this assertion at certain times). When traffic around a large city becomes congested and cumbersome, often a bypass is constructed to allow travelers to avoid the city as they travel.

Some of us take this same approach in our spiritual relationships. We want to strengthen our relationship with God, but sometimes other relationships get in the way. When a personal relationship becomes too complicated, demanding, time-consuming, or otherwise dysfunctional, we may try to bypass that person in our eagerness to get closer to God.

Our spiritual relationships, however, can't be like that. Though we may try to disconnect our unpleasant relationships with people from our desired relationship with God, Jesus said those relationships are inextricably connected. God does not want our offering when we know one of our personal relationships is in need of immediate attention. John emphasized the same point, but not as tactfully: "Whoever claims to love God yet hates a brother or sister is a liar" (1 John 4:20).

There is no quick pass to God. The road to spiritual growth often leads through messy personal relationships that are essential for us to address.

"This Thursday night at 7 pm . . .
the Fellowship Committee is hosting
its annual Masquerade Party
to promote genuine relationships in the church."

Who Was That Unmasked Man?

Here truly is an Israelite in whom there is no deceit.
John 1:47

According to recent estimates, Americans spend about $9 billion annually on Halloween. Over a third of that total goes toward costumes.

Many people live behind a mask most days of the year—not just on Halloween. It has become second nature for many of us to "put on a good face" when we go to school, work, or—sadly—church. We avoid revealing our flaws or weaknesses to others, and we usually don't share them voluntarily. As a result, we never receive encouragement or help to get better or stronger.

Tragically, self-imposed isolation is rampant. There are thousands and thousands of lonely people who, instead of admitting the truth and finding support from others like themselves, pretend that everything is just fine.

When Jesus first met Nathanael, who would become an apostle, Jesus identified him as someone "in whom there is no deceit." That trait alone made Nathanael stand out from many others around him.

It can also make us stand out. If we take off our masks and drop the phoniness and pretense, people will notice and respond. And so will God.

Bob and Nadine first noticed that their new church
tended to be judgmental during the Piano Prelude.

FLETCHER

Something in Your Eye?

Do not judge, or you too will be judged.
Matthew 7:1

Judgment. It used to be a potentially fear-inspiring word in a spiritual context. Yet recently judgment has become a regular—and accepted—part of life. Social media sites ask for your judgment on recent postings. Restaurants and hotels emphasize "Your opinion is important to us" as they seek a review of your recent visit. Televised talent shows invite viewers to judge which contestants continue and which ones are eliminated.

It can be fun to be a judge, wielding a degree of power over a person or situation. We might even revel in thinking that our opinions matter to other people. If we're not careful, however, we might carry that mentality into the church and other relationships where judgment should take a back seat to truth and service to others.

Jesus painted a tragicomic picture of someone attempting to remove a speck of sawdust from another person's eye while living with a plank in his own eye. Jesus's point was obvious, but he stated it anyway: "You hypocrite, first take the plank out of your own eye, and then you will see clearly to remove the speck from your brother's eye" (Matthew 7:5).

It's okay to use your wisdom and experience to clarify someone else's vision. Don't forget, however, to begin with yourself.

"If they don't have an adult Sunday School class,
we'll just have to put up with an immature one."

Got Milk? (Tsk, Tsk)

I gave you milk, not solid food, for you were not yet ready for it. . . . You are still worldly.

1 Corinthians 3:2–3

Know your audience is one of the primary rules for public speaking. If, for example, you were asked to talk on "Showing Greater Intimacy with Others," it would help to know whether your listeners were preschoolers, newlyweds, church congregants, or a group of hardened inmates. If you prepared for one of those groups but a different one showed up, you would probably need to make considerable adjustments on the fly.

Such was the case with Paul. The church in Corinth had a host of problems. Paul helped them get on track so they could run a good spiritual race, but they were still crawling! Two of their problems were jealousy and quarreling. They even argued about whether Paul or another person was the better leader (1 Corinthians 3:1–9).

Paul pointed out they had a worldly mentality, not a spiritual one. While Paul was eager to see the church unify and grow, their persistent immaturity—their desire for spiritual milk—stalled their growth, so they blamed Paul.

How often do we allow worldliness to short-circuit our spiritual growth? That's something to chew on. Or perhaps we need a sippy cup instead.

"I prefer to have minimal involvement in the church . . .
This morning, I'll be singing every other word."

Hole-Hearted Devotion

Love the Lord your God with all your heart and with all your soul and with all your strength and with all your mind.

Luke 10:27

Spiritual growth is very simple at its essence: receive God's love and forgiveness, and love him in return. It's so simple, in fact, that at times we might become a bit presumptuous. *Of course I love God! . . . Don't I?*

On one occasion Jesus defined more precisely what the challenge is for believers. As it turns out, loving God is not merely a spiritual (soul) matter. It also includes emotional (heart), physical (strength), and intellectual (mind) aspects. It's broader than we may realize. It's also more intensive, demanding *all* of us: heart, soul, strength, and mind.

Sometimes believers get half-hearted in some of those areas, but that's not usually the problem. More often, we get "hole-hearted": some of the wholehearted love and attention we should devote to God leaks out and is directed to other pursuits. Those involvements are not necessarily bad; they're just not as beneficial as total devotion to God. When we give him our complete love and attention, all the other incidentals of life fall into place.

We would do well to conduct a regular spiritual heart checkup. If we find holes, we should attend to them immediately so we can love God wholeheartedly. "Do this," Jesus said, "and you will live" (Luke 10:28). And, oh, what a life it can be.

Do You Hear What I Hear?

> You will be ever hearing but never understanding.
> Matthew 13:14

Jesus once cited Isaiah (6:9) to warn of the danger of closing our ears to spiritual truth. While we may hear clearly what is being taught, some of us lack the willingness to respond. Even we who do respond to Christ can have certain hearing issues.

One common problem is our tendency to hear what we want to hear. For example, what comes to mind when you hear the following words?

Fundamentalist　　Liberal　　Democrat　Republican　Roman Catholic

Southern Baptist　Immigrant　　Atheist　　Muslim　　Christian

Most of these words loosely define hundreds of thousands of individuals. Even so, we often view everyone in any of those particular groups with the same—often extremely exaggerated—stereotype. The stronger our personal views, the more likely we will see each of the groups either as allies or adversaries. Thus, when we encounter them, we may take a defensive position to protect our beliefs or go on the offense with outspoken rants of opposition.

All the groups in that list have something in common, however. Every person in every group is someone created in the image of God. It's unwise to pass unfounded and sweeping judgments on an individual based on "hair-trigger hearing" of the person's political views, denomination, or religion while ignoring the other aspects of the individual's character and worth. Given time, the Spirit may provide discernment and insight we don't have when we respond too hastily.

Rather than hearing what we want to hear, let's listen closer for God's clear voice of love and concern for those created in his image.

"During today's sermon,
I got a glimpse of our congregation's future,
and was shocked at just how much you had aged."

23

Future Shock Absorbers

I am convinced that neither death nor life, neither angels nor demons, neither the present nor the future . . . will be able to separate us from the love of God that is in Christ Jesus our Lord.

Romans 8:38–39

Why do so many people fear the future? Each generation seems to look down the road a few years and predict the world will get worse rather than better. Alvin Toffler's *Future Shock*[1] was a peek into an uncertain future that unsettled many of its six million or so readers. Prophecy books seem to be perpetual bestsellers—the more doom and gloom, the better.

Usually when God sent a prophet, the messenger had a dire warning about the future—if things didn't change. Yet where God is involved, a forthcoming unpleasant situation is never the end. God sees beyond coming exiles, beyond sieges and destruction, and beyond terrible wars and earthquakes; he assures his people of restoration and renewal. That's why letters in Revelation—with descriptions of horrific beasts, Armageddon, hundred-pound hailstones, and martyrs—were sent to seven churches as an *encouragement*. The unmistakable truth of the book of Revelation is that God is in control, Jesus is coming soon, and God's people can look forward to a new heaven, a new earth, and an as-yet-unrealized intimacy with him.

You may not be able to influence the future of the world to any degree, but you have much to say about *your* future. If you cling to God's inseparable love, you have nothing to fear.

24

Running, but Which Way?

Let us run with perseverance the race marked out for us.

Hebrews 12:1

Running is an interesting word. It normally means hurrying to get somewhere, yet when your car's engine is running, it can be burning fuel and making noise without going anywhere. Is it possible for us to think we're "running the race" when we're really stuck in park?

When used in a spiritual sense, *running* needs to be assessed in terms of speed and direction. We are commanded to "run with perseverance," so we can't race at full speed for long without burning out. Each believer must find a reasonable pace. In fact, God created the Sabbath so we can slow down and remember what's most important.

Sometimes we get turned around, whether intentionally or not. We may be like Jonah, who received clear directions from God and then started running in the opposite direction (Jonah 1). Or we may be like Elijah, who ran in fear from a personal crisis, only to discover he was running toward a much-needed quiet retreat with God (1 Kings 19:1–18).

While we're running around in all directions, God is on the move as well. Francis Thompson, a nineteenth-century English poet, wrote a thought-provoking poem depicting God as "The Hound of Heaven" in relentless pursuit of someone running away from him.

Your direction is just as important as your exertion. First determine your purpose and set your course. Then run with joy until you can celebrate at the finish line.

"His sermon on self-denial would have been more compelling had he placed more emphasis on what's in it for me."

25

Give It Up!

> Whoever wants to be my disciple must deny themselves and take up their cross daily and follow me.
>
> Luke 9:23

Daily self-denial. That's quite a price to pay to be a disciple, isn't it?

Yet that's exactly what Jesus modeled for us. The fact that he was on earth among human beings, having left his exalted position in heaven with his Father, was an unprecedented act of self-denial. And though he was God walking among us, he never put his desires above others' needs.

Jesus never expects us to do anything he hasn't already done, so it's really not too much for him to ask us to deny ourselves and "take up [our] cross." Although self-denial never comes easily, Jesus assures us that following his example will not become a burden (Matthew 11:28–30).

There's always something new and tantalizing we want. Thus we may perceive self-denial as an obstacle to joy and personal satisfaction. Yet a lack of self-denial has led to all kinds of health, financial, and relationship problems for many people.

Jesus's exemplary act of self-denial had an eventual payoff: "God exalted him to the highest place and gave him the name that is above every name" (Philippians 2:9). Now he invites us to join him in an earthly ministry with heavenly rewards.

What could you possibly want that would remotely compare to that?

"... Someone on the E-Ministry Committtee ... informing you that the Notification Committee has announced that the Scheduling Committee has canceled tonight's Finance Committee."

26

(Very) Small-Group Ministry

If you can find but one person who deals honestly and seeks
the truth, I will forgive this city.

Jeremiah 5:1

You may have heard this old joke: a committee is a group of people
who individually can do nothing, but when in a group, they are able to
determine that nothing can be done. When it comes to church committees, there is no shortage of jokes, yet many people have found
nothing funny at all about serving on them.

Ideally, a group of people should be able to come together with their
distinctive, Spirit-given gifts to arrive at ideas and creative solutions
that no single person could supply alone. Theoretically, a committee is
also a good starting point where someone new to the church can find
an area of productive and fulfilling ministry. Sadly, not all committee
work has such positive results.

Too often, committees waste people's time due to unclear agen-
das and small talk. Other times when something needs to be done,
the members just stare at one another and wait for someone else
to volunteer. When no one does, the item is tabled until the next
meeting—and the next.

One solitary individual might never resolve all the problems of dysfunctional church committees, but that shouldn't stop you from trying.
One person's light, when shining for God's kingdom, can illuminate a
world of darkness.

"Good . . . The next step is to deny self <u>without</u> posting it on Facebook."

27

What's Your Number?

Be careful not to practice your righteousness in front of others to be seen by them.

Matthew 6:1

Many people attempt to measure their effectiveness, popularity, or worth with a number: likes on Facebook, followers on Twitter, viewers on YouTube, and so forth. The bigger the number, the better. If they're comparing responses to potato salad recipes, cute kitty videos, or recent vacation photos, there's really no harm done.

It is tempting and problematic, however, to take the same approach related to spiritual growth and disciplines. When we pray in public places, give money to worthwhile causes, or do other good deeds, do we subconsciously sneak a peek to see how many likes we're getting from nearby observers?

Os Guinness, in his book *The Call*, revisits an old concept known as "The Audience of One."[1] The Puritans and others sought to disregard what anyone other than God thought of them. Spiritual disciplines remain secret because God sees, so that is the only concern. Decisions are made based on what Christ would do in a situation, regardless of popular opinion.

What's *your* number? Who is *your* audience? It might feel lonely at first when you stop appealing to the masses. But as you live to please an Audience of One, you'll soon discover nothing is more liberating.

"I haven't felt God's presence in the service
since they switched the bulletin font to Helvetica."

No Excuse

> But Moses said, "Pardon your servant, Lord. Please send someone else."
>
> Exodus 4:13

Many of us create excuses to keep a bit of distance between God and us. After all, if we get too close, he might ask us to do something impossible. Perhaps not impossible, but herculean. Or at least he might ask us to do something inconvenient.

The sooner we get rid of our excuses and do what God says, the better off we'll be. When God gave Moses an assignment at the burning bush, the prince-turned-shepherd was a master excuse giver: "I'm a nobody. . . . The Israelites may not believe me. . . . I'm a really lousy public speaker. . . . I'd really rather you sent someone else" (Exodus 3–4). But Moses finally consented, obeyed, and became one of Israel's most memorable heroes.

The people in Jesus's parable of the great banquet (Luke 14:15–24) were just as adept at making excuses: "New field . . . new cows . . . new wife. We can't be bothered right now." But in that case, their excuses caused them to miss out on a marvelous banquet—a symbol of all the wonderful spiritual blessings only God can provide.

Failure to respond to God may stem from insecurity, stubbornness, fear, laziness, or other reasons—none of which are valid. If we don't get past our excuses and trust God to put us where he wants us, we may see the best things in life, but we will be looking from a distance.

"I told you not to ask Howard for spiritual direction."

29

Who You Gonna Call?

The wisdom of this world is foolishness in God's sight.
1 Corinthians 3:19

How do you make a difficult decision? People try a variety of options: Flip a coin. Try "Eeny, meeny, miny, moe." See what a fortune cookie advises. Check the horoscope. Consult a fortune-teller. If all else fails, look at the Magic 8-Ball, still selling about a million per year after being introduced in the late 1940s. Some of these methods we take so casually were forbidden under Mosaic law (Leviticus 19:26, 31) because they steered people away from God.

One of the premier advisors of the Old Testament was a man named Ahithophel, a consultant to King David. One Bible paraphrase states that the advice Ahithophel gave "was treated as if God himself had spoken" (2 Samuel 16:23 MESSAGE). When Absalom tried to usurp his father's throne, he recruited Ahithophel but then rejected Ahithophel's battle strategy. So much for human wisdom. Ahithophel saw with certainty that Absalom's attempted coup was already lost, so to avoid future reprisals from David, he went home and hanged himself (2 Samuel 17:1–23).

It never hurts to seek someone's advice for input or confirmation when making a difficult decision. But believers have the Holy Spirit, who provides "the mind of Christ" (1 Corinthians 2:15–16). He should always be our primary source of wisdom. Yet even heaven-sent advice doesn't do much good without the human will to follow it.

"I no longer simply talk the talk . . . Sometimes, I tweet."

30

What Would Jesus Tweet?

The crowds learned [where Jesus was] and followed him. He welcomed them and spoke to them about the kingdom of God, and healed those who needed healing.

Luke 9:11

When TV preachers began to promote the "prosperity gospel" while looking and dressing the part, a late-'80s song asked the piercing question: "Would Jesus Wear a Rolex?" It was a facetious but somewhat thought-provoking question. A similar question currently being posed on the internet is "What would Jesus tweet?" Another is even more basic: "How would Jesus use social media?"

We can speculate to our heart's content, but we would do well to also consider what made Jesus such an effective communicator when he had such limited "technology" at his disposal. He taught truth, provided fresh insight into God, and consistently demonstrated grace and compassion. His relationships were personal. He looked into people's eyes. He touched lepers, picked up small children, summoned seekers to come down from trees (Luke 19:1–10), and shared meals with sinners, to the great dismay of his critics. He proved he had the capability of healing people long-distance if needed (Matthew 8:5–13), but he didn't do that very often.

Personal concern and attention are still crucial to effective ministry. Social media allows us to reach great numbers of people in an instant, but let's never lose the personal touch. We may never know what Jesus would tweet to the masses, but we know how he would respond to a hurting person in front of him. And he tells us to go and do likewise.

"So far, the committee to explore our lack of demographic diversity includes Uncle Marvin, Aunt Virginia, Uncle Wesley, our cousin Raymond, your two sisters . . . and, of course, Grandpa."

31

Extended Family

God sets the lonely in families.
Psalm 68:6

When a relatively normal family (if such a thing exists) gets together at home, they usually tolerate one another's eccentricities and peculiarities. Natural chatterboxes talk at will while the introverts quietly go about their interests. No one bothers Grandma when her show comes on. Everyone contributes to the family dynamics in their own unique ways.

But when those individuals go outside the home, their behavior (and peace of mind) may change drastically. At school, talkative children are pressured to keep quiet while the shy ones are prodded to speak up. At work, teens and adults might feel insecure or self-conscious, especially if they receive stern glances or judgmental comments.

The church is supposed to be different. Churches should create environments that embrace people of all ages, personalities, ethnic backgrounds, and reputations. We should be a "family of believers" (Galatians 6:10) that welcomes overworked parents, hyperactive kids, cranky grandparents, crying babies, spinster aunts, and crazy uncles—along with those of us who are perfectly normal. Keep in mind, however, that any group comprised of human beings can at times be dysfunctional. When that happens, people sometimes criticize or leave churches for being too liberal, too judgmental, too modern, too old-fashioned, or something else.

Let's not be too quick to condemn or abandon our church families. None of us are sinless or flawless, so we will be right at home with others who are a lot like us.

"Involvement in a new church should be gradual . . .
For the first year, let's limit our sermon complaints to three
and question the Pastor's motives maybe once or twice."

32

Welcome to Our Church. Watch Your Back.

> I appeal to you . . . in the name of our Lord Jesus Christ, that all of you agree with one another in what you say and that there be no divisions among you.
>
> 1 Corinthians 1:10

It was a church where people arrived early . . . so they could pig out at the Communion table before all the food was gone and get a good buzz before worship started. You could take your new wife, even if she had been your stepmother last year. Church members were suing one another in secular courts (1 Corinthians 5–6; 11). It was a church that might have benefited more from a bouncer or referee than a pastor.

Paul tried his best to resolve the many problems at the church in Corinth. He didn't dodge the challenging issues; he addressed each one with logic and spiritual wisdom. There were also other problems in the church. Members emphatically supported different church leaders, bickering about which one was best. They developed holier-than-thou attitudes over issues that weren't crucial to their faith. They wanted to pick and choose which spiritual gifts they received, they didn't utilize their gifts for the good of the church, and they didn't exercise their gifts with love. They weren't unified about doctrine, appropriate dress, or many other issues.

Ouch. Those sound like contemporary problems. Church unity requires members to eliminate criticism, gossip, competition, and moral indifference. Church leaders can appeal for these higher standards, but will they bring positive change? That depends on the attitudes and actions of each person sitting in the pews.

"So . . . that's four votes to approve the minutes
and one vote to simply tolerate them."

33

Weight Problems

Do not have two differing weights in your bag—one heavy, one light.

Deuteronomy 25:13

Among the many rules and regulations tucked into Old Testament law was a prohibition against misrepresentation in financial transactions. Dishonest merchants were known to keep two sets of weights. If they were buying something by the pound, they would use the weights that provided a lower total. If they were selling, however, a different set of weights would add a few more ounces for extra profit.

God calls for transparency in *all* our dealings with others—not just in buying and selling. Sometimes the problem is not so much intentional deceit as it is a skewed sense of self-importance. For example, if we believe ourselves to be weighty and irreplaceable members of our spiritual community, we may have an exaggerated sense of self-worth. The truth is that instead of being the anchor that secures the ship (as we suppose), we're really just dead weight that drags the ground and hinders the ship's forward progress.

We would do well to acknowledge and affirm that Christ alone is the cornerstone, the rock, the fortress, and the anchor holding the church together. When we take ourselves too seriously, we start throwing our weight around. A much better option is to lighten up.

"After you sign the no-hugging covenant,
we'll get you a name tag, some chili,
and introduce you to the rest of the guys."

34

Greetings

Greet one another with a holy kiss.
Romans 16:16

Many natural extroverts have no idea how distressing it can be for introverts to respond to some of the commands of Scripture. Evangelism is one of the biggest challenges: "Hey, let's all go tell strangers about some of our most intimate experiences with God!" Such tasks are more than a little intimidating for individuals who can hardly make eye contact with people they don't know.

Even something as simple as saying hello and exchanging brief pleasantries during a church service can be an uncomfortable challenge for some, yet such greetings shouldn't be left to "professionals." All churchgoers need to be welcoming and accommodating to one another, especially to newcomers who are interested in the church. When someone feels accepted, he or she is usually more open to a second visit.

Eventually, we can learn to expand our greetings to other places we go. Most of us may never deliver a "holy kiss" to others, but it doesn't matter. A handshake, high five, fist bump, or hug in celebration of the love of Christ can also be holy—especially when accompanied by a warm and loving smile.

"When I heard you had removed me from the church roll,
I immediately jumped into my car,
punched the address into the GPS,
and drove over here!"

35

Membership Dues

You are no longer foreigners and strangers, but fellow citizens
with God's people and also members of his household.

Ephesians 2:19

Membership. This word means different things in different contexts.
If you're invited to be a member of a certain club, you might expect to
lounge around on overstuffed furniture and engage in repartee, while
attendants bring you the beverage of your choice. But if you're a member
of the Peace Corps, the PTA, or another service organization, you
don't anticipate exclusive benefits. You expect to throw your energy
and resources into conscientious work for the benefit of others.

So what does it mean to be a *church* member? Some people think
the church fits the first category. They go to receive inspiration from
the rapturous music, the uplifting messages, and the significant inter-
changes with fellow attendees. In time, however, they may see how
many people are involved in providing the music, the flowers, the re-
freshments, and all the other elements of worship they had been taking
for granted. It turns out those things don't just occur automatically;
people must sacrifice time and effort to make them happen each week.

It is a privilege to be a valued member of the body of Christ. Yet
church membership involves much more than what you *receive* every
Sunday morning; it includes your willingness to contribute your gifts
and resources for the good of the body.

In the long run, it's a pretty sweet deal. Membership is a lifelong
commitment, but the benefits continue long afterward.

"How did your sermon on Enduring Times of Suffering go?
I left about halfway through."

36

Competitive Suffering

The churning inside me never stops; days of suffering confront me.

Job 30:27

Has someone ever confided in you about a traumatic event he or she was undergoing and then you failed to respond in a helpful or encouraging way? Instead of listening patiently and offering a sympathetic ear, perhaps you quickly reacted by sharing a personal story of your own in an attempt to make a connection with or "one-up" the other person's trying circumstance.

Many of us go through life discovering new levels of suffering. A preteen girl's first rejection by a boy she likes is insignificant in the context of the world's suffering, but it's the worst pain she has yet endured. Later in life a divorce, bankruptcy, or job loss can seem like the end of the world. But then come deaths of loved ones, diagnoses of terrible diseases, and more. We may eventually learn that though our suffering is great, there are others who endure far worse.

Suffering attacks us in many ways, and it often brings pain, fear, loneliness, guilt, regret, anger, and hopelessness. Sometimes, like Job, we must endure suffering upon suffering with no adequate explanation. We naturally keep asking, "Why?"

Because we don't always get answers, wise people learn to use suffering as a catalyst. The apostle Paul noted, "We also glory in our sufferings, because we know that suffering produces perseverance; perseverance, character; and character, hope" (Romans 5:3–4).

Let's not compete to see who has it worst. Instead, let's see how quickly we can allow our sufferings to bring us closer to God.

"The back pew is meeting Thursday night to compose this month's,
'We can't hear the sermon' letter . . .
Pass it on."

37

Complaining vs. Problem-Solving

Do everything without grumbling or arguing, so that you may become blameless and pure, "children of God without fault in a warped and crooked generation."

Philippians 2:14–15

One episode of *The Simpsons* portrayed a parody of the Goldilocks story. Bart and Lisa walked into a house where they found three bowls of porridge. Bart found the first one too hot. The second was too cold. He shrugged and said, "Well, this doesn't take a genius." He then mixed them together and enjoyed both bowls. He resolved two long-standing complaints with one creative solution.

It's easy to complain, but complaining is an affront to God: "How long will this wicked community grumble against me? I have heard the complaints of these grumbling Israelites" (Numbers 14:27). God hears all our complaints, even those whispered in church parking lots or quiet corners of the break room. Complaints prevented an entire generation from being admitted into the promised land. They also keep us from receiving many of the good things God has to offer.

With a little patience, perseverance, and desire, bolstered with faith and prayer, we could find solutions to resolve most of our complaints. We could experience increased joy and peace. We could form stronger relationships with others. We could be better parents, friends, and co-workers.

Or we could just whine while waiting for someone else to take care of the problem.

"Come on, folks! . . . Put your hearts into it! . . . I can hardly hear you!"

38

Volume Control

For God does speak—now one way, now another—though no one perceives it.

Job 33:14

Sometimes God speaks in a such a way that no one can miss his message. When Elijah stood against 450 priests of Baal on Mount Carmel, he prayed for a clear sign so the observers would recognize the God of Israel. God responded with a heavenly firestorm that devoured Elijah's sacrifice, altar and all (1 Kings 18:36–39). Not one of the startled Israelites ignored God's message.

Yet Elijah's boldness incited the wrath of Queen Jezebel, who swore he would be dead within a day. Elijah ran for his life and hid in the wilderness, waiting to hear from God. There he witnessed a "great and powerful wind" that tore mountains apart, followed by an earthquake and then a fire. Yet God did not speak from any of those fearsome natural phenomena. Instead, he reassured and encouraged his prophet through "a gentle whisper" (1 Kings 19:1–18).

God spoke to Moses from a burning bush (Exodus 3) and to Job out of a storm (Job 38:1). But if we listen for him only in dramatic presentations, we will miss much, if not most, of what he has to say. Often we are hindered by the noise and static on our end. If we regularly find a quiet time and place to listen, however, the soft-spoken truth of God usually comes through loud and clear.

"Ever feel like your prayers go right to voice mail?"

Maybe God Will Hear

> But as for me, I watch in hope for the LORD, I wait for God my
> Savior; my God will hear me.
>
> Micah 7:7

Perhaps you've heard people say they didn't think their prayers were getting above the ceiling. Maybe you've thought the same thing. Most of us experience situations where we are motivated to pray more from desperation than from faith.

Hezekiah was one of the few decent kings among the dozens who ruled Israel and Judah. During his reign, a ruthless Assyrian commander named Sennacherib appeared to be an unstoppable force headed his way. Assyrian messengers publicly announced that Jerusalem would be the next city to fall, and that resistance was futile (Isaiah 36). The situation appeared grim, so Hezekiah sent word to Isaiah, hoping that God would "hear the words of the field commander" and do something to avert the threat (Isaiah 37:1-4).

Isaiah sent back a confident reply telling Hezekiah not to worry. He said God would cause Sennacherib to pack up and go home. Sure enough, the next morning 185,000 Assyrian soldiers were found dead because of an angel of the Lord. Sennacherib was soon dead as well (Isaiah 37:36-38).

Not long afterward, another desperate prayer of Hezekiah's added fifteen years to his life (Isaiah 38:1-8). Take it from King Hezekiah: even when you're uncertain, distraught, or fearful, God hears your prayers and he responds.

"The Pastor keeps referring to
'this morning's text' . . .
But which one?"

40

Not Speaking the Same Language?

All the believers were together and had everything in common.

Acts 2:44

Recent statistics from United States high school graduates who had been active in their churches indicate that two-thirds of them stopped attending church for at least a year between the ages of eighteen and twenty-two. The church dropouts listed various reasons for their departure, but 71 percent said they had not planned on leaving.

Some people claim the church doesn't speak the language of the younger generation. It's an understandable complaint. Young people are always creating words and phrases that distinguish their generation, and language can be a powerfully divisive problem. (Any tourist who's been lost or in need of a bathroom in a foreign country can confirm this.) Sometimes God creates these divisions. When humanity became way too arrogant at the Tower of Babel, God "confused" their common language, and they went their separate ways (Genesis 11:1–9).

But God can also bridge communication gaps created by different languages. After the Holy Spirit descended on the day of Pentecost, the Galilean believers in Jerusalem began to declare the wonders of God in the languages of everyone in attendance—people from all over the world (Acts 2:1–12).

So don't be reluctant to strike up a conversation with fellow believers who may be considerably younger or older than you. They may *seem* to speak a different language, but if you seek to communicate with love, the Spirit of God will be there to translate.

"I just hope his sermon on the dangers of self-centeredness doesn't make us late for lunch."

41

Stomach Trouble

Many live as enemies of the cross of Christ. Their destiny is destruction, their god is their stomach, and their glory is in their shame.

Philippians 3:18–19

We've all been there. We're in church on a Sunday morning (perhaps after skipping breakfast to keep from being late again), trying to cope with a rumbling stomach, and planning what we'll get to eat as soon as the preacher finally stops talking.

While occasional daydreaming about lunch during worship is certainly not among the seven deadly sins, we should take action if our focus begins to shift. For example, if we have set aside the worship service as the one hour of the week we will devote ourselves to God, we should ensure he has our full attention for that short time.

This isn't a stomach problem; it's a heart problem. If your stomach regularly distracts your heart, one solution might be to eat *less*. Fasting has been a spiritual discipline for centuries; practitioners use hunger to turn their attention to God rather than to their favorite food.

While some people are avid advocates of fasting, it may not be for everyone. Yet if you ask yourself "What do I want for lunch today?" more often than "What does God want from me today?" it might be time to give fasting a try.

"I still think a kick line of heavenly host is a bit edgy for a Christmas pageant!"

42

Drawing the Line

I strive always to keep my conscience clear before God and man.

Acts 24:16

From the beginning of the church, growth and change have been problematic. Many early followers of Jesus were steeped in centuries of Jewish tradition and discipline; they opposed the inclusion of "god-less" Gentiles whom they felt were a threat to spiritual purity. While the believers' opinion was based on a strong commitment to God, they discovered it was God's will for them to adapt and worship together, and it was God's grace that enabled the change.

Even now we should extend God's grace to fellow believers who disagree with us on matters of personal conscience (Romans 14). Scripture makes clear, however, that God's abundant grace is not a ticket to adopt or accept an "anything goes" lifestyle. What if someone proudly flaunts an inappropriate sexual relationship in church? We should kick him out (1 Corinthians 5:1–5). What if self-serving leaders promote false doctrines? We should shut them up (1 Timothy 1:3–4).

Such problems are primarily for church leaders to resolve, yet *everyone* needs to determine where to draw the line when considering which issues constitute a genuine spiritual threat and which ones merely cause personal discomfort. When the day comes that "each of us will give an account of ourselves to God" (Romans 14:12), we won't be able to blame our action (or inaction) on church leaders.

Every person should prayerfully discern God's truth, separate it from personal opinion, and live accordingly. Only then can we experience the peace and joy that comes from having a clear conscience before God and others.

"... And please give Fred and Eugene and Joe and Ray
the maturity to understand that even some deeply devout men
find praying like this terribly uncomfortable."

43

Bond Like a Girl

Jonathan became one in spirit with David, and he loved him
as himself.

1 Samuel 18:1

Vulnerable. Transparent. Fragile. Unassertive. Masculine.

Which word doesn't belong on this list? Many people might be quick
to delete the final term. Despite the plethora of men's movements
that have arisen since the 1970s, masculinity is still narrowly defined
for many men.

People have no problem with women's groups revealing their deep-
est feelings, weeping together, offering lingering hugs, and so forth.
But if men exhibit such behaviors, onlookers often respond with stern
glances and excessive throat clearing.

Some people even feel uncomfortable discussing stories like that
of David and Jonathan, two men who "became one in spirit." Many
guys will admit (perhaps reluctantly) to having one or more friends
with whom they have formed a similar relationship, yet talking seriously about such masculine relationships might make them squirm.
Most have not forgotten the taunts they heard while growing up: "You
throw [or run or hit] like a girl!"

When Jesus said, "Blessed are the meek" (Matthew 5:5), he wasn't
being gender specific. Nor was he targeting one group of people with
the qualities he promoted—love, service, submission, compassion,
and so forth. In fact, Jesus was the ultimate model of those virtues,
and his strength of character was never in question. All of us—both
women *and* men—would be better people if we followed his example
more consistently.

"There's a grandfather clause in the church by-laws . . .
Any changes must be approved by my grandfather."

Wielding vs. Yielding

But you will receive power when the Holy Spirit comes on you.

Acts 1:8

We've all seen political figures, associates at work, or people in certain situations who rise to power and don't handle the responsibility very well. Often when someone is given the authority to do a job, he or she interprets it as the right to tell others what to do. And once some people get a little taste of such power, they immediately go overboard.

You'd think followers of God would know better, yet the church has more than its share of powermongers. In the first-century church, a magician who witnessed the power of God at work desperately wanted to purchase it, but he was severely reprimanded by the apostles (Acts 8:9–24). Even today there is no shortage of churches that seem to be more responsive to the will of an individual with money or influence than to the pastor or church board.

Believers can indeed expect power; it was one of Jesus's final promises before he returned to heaven. God empowers his people to correct, heal, encourage, and comfort, yet Jesus consistently demonstrated that such power was to be directed toward *others*, not for the benefit of self. If you find yourself desiring to wield God's power as a show of force, you've got a problem. But if you're yielding your personal time and resources to strengthen God's kingdom, more power to you!

"I hate it when these young pastors
use obscure theological phrases like,
'Free app for your tablet.'"

45

To Each His Own?

I have become all things to all people so that by all possible means I might save some.

1 Corinthians 9:22

Have you ever visited a church for the first time and felt incredibly uncomfortable? Maybe you felt like you didn't belong there or that the people were just too weird. Have guests in your church felt out of place?

With the vast number of church denominations, worship styles, and sizes to choose from, we can usually find a church where everyone looks like us, worships like us, and reads from the Bible translation we like. But is that what a church should be?

When the apostle Paul began to organize the first Christian churches, the only requirement was faith in Christ. He readily recruited Jews and Gentiles, males and females, slaves and free people (Galatians 3:28). They didn't have hundreds of churches to choose from; there was usually only one church in an area. The believers had to learn to sit beside one another, worship together, and work out any differences created by their backgrounds.

How can we follow Paul's example to be "all things to all people"? Do we care equally for successful businesspeople, hipsters, slackers, lonely seniors, single parents, the local homeless population, recovering addicts, and anyone else willing to pursue a growing relationship with Jesus? Ideally, churches should be a wonderful blend of all those subsets of people, learning together to share God's great love. When people come seeking a place in God's kingdom, we should make them feel welcome. But do we? Or do we go looking for another church where we will be more comfortable?

"When I started pouring out honest prayers to God,
I didn't receive immediate answers . . . Only
shocked silence for seven days."

46

Honest to God

Arise, LORD! Deliver me, my God! Strike all my enemies on the jaw; break the teeth of the wicked.

Psalm 3:7

Have you ever gently offered help to an angry child or teenager but received a curt response: "Nothing. I'm fine!"? Probably the more you tried to pry the truth from the child, the more withdrawn or angry he or she became.

If you've experienced this, try to imagine what God must feel like when his people who are grappling with all sorts of turbulent and troubling emotions pray to him with flowery expressions of praise through gritted teeth, as if he doesn't know what we're really thinking and feeling. How can we sustain or improve *any* relationship when we are not honest with the other person?

David and the other psalmists weren't shy about telling God how they really felt. The psalms are filled with generous and abundant praise and gratitude, yet interspersed among those positive expressions are admissions of anger, rage, jealousy, confusion, doubt, calls for retribution, and more. Jesus turned to the Psalms on the cross when he wondered, "My God, my God, why have you forsaken me?" (Psalm 22:1; Matthew 27:46).

We might stop short of asking God to break the teeth of our enemies, yet we should take comfort that he hears and welcomes our honest prayers—whether expressing grateful worship or grasping for understanding. He won't be surprised by anything you tell him, so why not be honest with God? If nothing else, it will help you start being more honest with yourself.

"No Wi-Fi . . . Pass it on . . ."

47

A Nice Place to Visit, But . . .

"[God] will wipe every tear from their eyes. There will be no more death" or mourning or crying or pain.

Revelation 21:4

Nothing is ever good enough for some people. They read about heaven's streets of gold and pearly gates (Revelation 21–22) and respond, "Wouldn't that get boring?" They yawn when they imagine sitting around on a cloud, eternally strumming a harp.

Maybe they are jaded because they have seen people who tried to establish "heaven on earth" environments before, each attempt an epic fail. The book of Ecclesiastes tells of a wealthy and powerful figure (perhaps Solomon) who threw himself into work projects, sumptuous living, the pursuit of wisdom, and more, only to conclude that "everything is meaningless" (Ecclesiastes 1:2). We often hear the same from seemingly successful people who appear to "have it all" yet are never happy. Is that what's in store for all of us in heaven?

If we come to that conclusion, we're missing the point. The attraction of heaven is not the gold or the pearls; it's the glory of God. Most of us have had rare and treasured occasions when we were with someone in a perfect moment that we desperately hoped would never end, but it did. And it always does. Yet if we could take away death, pain, time, and sin, and then envision such a moment, what might it be like to share that level of intimacy with *everyone*, in the presence of God, forever?

When God finally shows us life as he always intended it to be, no one will be yawning. That's impossible to do when your jaw has hit the ground.

"I admit, I don't pray as much as I used to . . .
I assume God is reading my blog."

48

Make That Call

The LORD is near to all who call on him, to all who call on him in truth.

Psalm 145:18

If God knows everything we need and all we're thinking, why do we need to pray?

This question comes up quite frequently. It crosses many of our minds. We believe God is omniscient, so why doesn't he just read our thoughts and respond?

After giving the matter more thought, most people realize such a concept of prayer is shortsighted; it potentially leads to ignoring God. Do we really expect prayer to be equivalent to "Close your eyes, make a wish, and wait for it to come true"? We shouldn't even bother *asking*?

For one thing, prayer should be much more than reciting a list of things we want. Prayer should be communication between two parties in a growing relationship. A man can believe his wife knows he loves her, but he would be quite callous to stop saying so. An aging widow can believe her adult daughter cares about her, but she still looks forward to every phone call and opportunity to catch up with the grandkids. We don't take such relationships for granted.

In addition to maintaining and strengthening a relationship with God, prayer helps us to see our world from his perspective. While God already knows what we're thinking, through prayer we begin to discover his thoughts (Isaiah 55:8–9). So call on him. Lines are always open.

"Pastor Tim spends too much time on Facebook . . .
At tonight's meeting, he tired to 'un-elder' me."

49

Breaking Up Ain't Hard to Do

Give careful thought to the paths for your feet and be steadfast in all your ways.

Proverbs 4:26

Social media has made it easier than ever to connect with other people. You get an online request, click a button, and you've got a new friend! Before you know it, your friend list grows from dozens to hundreds of names.

The other side of the coin, however, is that it's just as easy to disconnect. If one of your hundreds of friends does something to displease you, all it takes is another click of a button and that person ceases to exist—at least in your media world. And truthfully, if the "friend" is little more than a stranger's name on a list, that can hardly be classified as a genuine relationship.

The problem, though, is the temptation to become just as casual and unattached in real-life friendships. If severing a connection happens whenever someone we care about reprimands us, appears to ignore us for too long, expresses a political opinion we disagree with, or commits a similar slight, that's a problem.

Scripture calls believers to be "steadfast in all [our] ways." Steadfastness involves an unwavering commitment to patience, perseverance, faith, and loyalty. When steadfast friends face problems or disagreements, they don't click a button to *dis*connect; they make a call, work out the problem, and *re*connect. It's rarely a fast fix, but a steadfast fix will make the relationship stronger than ever.

"This sermon series on spiritual maturity is exactly what this congregation needs!"

50

Better Hopes and Gardens

Let perseverance finish its work so that you may be mature and complete, not lacking anything.

James 1:4

Believe it or not, at one time there was no such thing as "fast food." Most families planted and tended vegetable gardens. Long weeks would pass between putting a seed in the ground and picking something good to eat. During that time, growers had to contend with late freezes, long periods of too-dry or too-wet conditions, destructive bugs and other critters, and a host of other problems.

By necessity, growers learned lessons of patience and perseverance. Even after kids could finally see the green tops popping out of the ground, they couldn't be too eager to yank out a ripe radish or carrot. It took a lot of waiting before the fruit or vegetable was *mature*—ripe and ready.

So it is with *spiritual* growth. There is no fast track to spiritual maturity; the only route that gets us there begins with challenge. That's why James began his letter with a statement that confounds so many of us: "Consider it pure joy . . . whenever you face trials of many kinds" (James 1:2). It's a strange joyride, to be sure. Yet our hurts, disappointments, pains, and sufferings teach us perseverance—the primary prerequisite for maturity.

The seed of perseverance, once planted, can take a long time to mature, but its resulting fruit is the joy of an ever-maturing relationship with our loving God. It's well worth the wait.

"Since the Pastor couldn't make it tonight's small group,
we'll have to skip the opening and closing prayers,
and the lesson on the importance of active lay people in the church."

51

Welcome to the Priesthood

You . . . are being built into a spiritual house to be a holy priesthood.

1 Peter 2:5

Christianity was never intended to be a spectator sport. Faith in Christ has always been a call to action. Originally, it involved joining a community of believers and investing time and resources into their well-being *every day*. That's a far cry from today's tendency to show up at church a few times each month and hope a speaker will somehow inspire us to be better people.

Pastors were eventually called to teach and shepherd various congregations, but they were never expected do all the work of the church. Peter explained that *all* followers of Christ are considered priests and share priestly duties!

What are those duties? Surprisingly enough, we are still to offer sacrifices: each of us should offer ourselves as a living sacrifice to God (Romans 12:1), and we are to continually offer a sacrifice of praise to him (Hebrews 13:15). We are also expected to hear one another's confessions (James 5:16). Other duties include loving our fellow believers (2 Thessalonians 1:3), praying for them (Ephesians 6:18), and encouraging them (1 Thessalonians 5:11).

In addition to being spiritual advisors, Old Testament priests had many other responsibilities: butchering meat for sacrifices, building altars, crafting special furniture and clothing, and serving as medical and legal authorities. We have it easy in comparison, but it can't all be done with just a once-a-week, one-hour commitment. It's time to roll up the sleeves of your robe, fellow priest. There's work to be done.

"Our congregation is an older demographic . . .
The average age in our youth group is thirty-two."

52

No Need to Show Your ID

Do not let anyone look down on you because you are young,
but set an example for the believers in speech, in conduct, in
love, in faith and in purity.

1 Timothy 4:12

We sometimes make presumptions about people solely based on their age. *Some people are simply too young to do certain things,* we think, but then we see a preteen prodigy perform a classical masterpiece on a talent show and our opinions shift a bit. *Maybe it's time for Junior to start those piano lessons after all.* Or we see where an octogenarian has just climbed Mount Everest, and we ponder, *Maybe Grandpa isn't ready for the retirement home just yet.*

Of course, it *does* usually take several years for a young person to acquire professional vocal or instrumental proficiency. And normally, physical decline slows down or halts certain physical activities as we age. Yet *spiritual* activity is not so age-restrictive. Paul encouraged his young protégé, Timothy, to pastor an older congregation. Goliath's judgment of David as "little more than a boy" (1 Samuel 17:42) turned out to be a fatal mistake.

At the other end of the age spectrum, Abraham was one hundred and Sarah was ninety when they became parents, and they laughed at the thought right up to the labor pains. Elizabeth became the mother of John the Baptist at an advanced age as well. And God didn't even call Moses at the burning bush until the reluctant fugitive was eighty.

Your age should never be an excuse to avoid working for God. Whether you are old or young, get going. You're setting an example for the rest of us!

"Okay . . . heads . . . we hire a church consultant to help us update our organizational decision making process . . ."

53

Don't Just Stand There

The LORD said to Moses, "Why are you crying out to me? Tell the Israelites to move on."

Exodus 14:15

Conscientious believers sometimes agonize over determining God's will for their lives. It's certainly an issue worthy of much thought. But what are we to do if we just can't discern the best course of action?

Often our best option is to do *something*. We might not know God's will for a *specific* situation, but we have a clear knowledge of his general will for his people. Jesus said our priorities are to love God with all our heart, soul, strength, and mind, and to love our neighbors as ourselves (Luke 10:27). That's always a good starting point for our actions. Sometimes God waits for us to make a move before he provides more specifics about what to do.

When the panicky Israelites stood staring at the Red Sea before them and glancing over their shoulders at the rapidly approaching Egyptian army, Moses didn't need to ponder God's will; God told him to get going. More specifically, he commanded, "Raise your staff and stretch out your hand over the sea to divide the water so that the Israelites can go through the sea on dry ground" (Exodus 14:16).

When you aren't sure exactly what to do, don't overthink it. Don't just stand there. Do *something*. In most cases, that action will be what it takes to help you get back in step with God's will for your life.

"Our church needs forward-thinking leaders . . . like we had in 1959."

54

Look Both Ways

Since we are surrounded by such a great cloud of witnesses, let us . . . [fix] our eyes on Jesus, the pioneer and perfecter of faith. For the joy set before him he endured the cross.

Hebrews 12:1–2

Among the dozens of Roman gods was one named Janus, who was known as the god of beginnings, transitions, and passages. As such, he was usually portrayed with two faces: one looking to the past, and one to the future.

The author of Hebrews reminds us that our God is eternal, timeless, and ever-present. Even so, he wants his time-bound people to be more cognizant of where they have been and where they are going. He encourages us to maintain a dual perspective: we look back in gratitude, and we look forward in faith.

Hebrews 11 lists an assortment of God's faithful people, briefly recalling their remarkable challenges and accomplishments. But the lengthy list concludes with the observation that none of those exemplary people saw the Messiah they had been promised. Hebrews 12 portrays that faithful group as an exuberant crowd in a stadium, cheering on believers who are still running the race. As we run toward our Savior at the finish line, we continue what they started.

Some of us fondly dwell on "the good old days" with our past accomplishments. Others have more of a fervent focus on the future, determined to make the most of whatever lies ahead. If we learn to look both ways, the new perspective doubles our reasons for gratitude and makes each new day a meaningful adventure.

Until he stepped into the men's room, Larry didn't realize just how personal joining a family church could be.

55

Think Small

Truly I tell you that if two of you on earth agree about anything they ask for, it will be done for them by my Father in heaven.

Matthew 18:19

Bigger is better, or so they say. That appears to be the unspoken standard for churches these days. A crowd of hundreds or thousands can certainly generate much energy and enthusiasm when packed into an expansive arena or church sanctuary.

Yet the success of a church of any size usually depends on the closeness and number of its small groups. The early church modeled that for us. As their numbers grew rapidly—from 120 to beyond 3,000 to over 5,000 (Acts 1:15; 2:41; 4:4)—they had no place large enough for everyone to assemble. They met instead in house churches—small groups—that helped new believers share with one another, learn together, grow spiritually, and thrive.

Small groups are still powerful ways for believers to bond as they cultivate a greater love for God and one another. Caution must be exercised, however, to prevent such closeness from becoming a clique (akin to school students in the lunchroom cafeteria). In addition, if we lose sight of the unity Christ desires, small groups can become competitive or even adversarial (1 Corinthians 1:10–17).

If you're starting to feel lost in a big church, give small groups a try. If one isn't readily available, start one. All it takes is two people in agreement with Jesus to make progress, so you're already halfway there.

56

Tend to Your Own Business

Lord, what about him?
John 21:21

The internet has helped us connect with thousands or millions of other people in cyberspace. Because anything remotely interesting can go viral in a matter of hours, we're able to poke our cyber-noses into lots of other people's business. Their experiences seem much more intriguing than our own.

Parents and teachers all witness the same phenomenon on a smaller scale. When making assignments, they may try to design different challenges that will be appropriate for specific individuals. But when siblings or students realize someone else is getting a different assignment, they tend to respond, "Why doesn't that other person have to do the same thing?"

We instinctively want work assignments, rewards, and punishments to be exactly the same for everyone. That *sounds* right, until we realize God intentionally didn't create everyone exactly alike. Consequently, it would be unfair to expect everyone to have the same satisfaction or challenge from the same assignment.

Even Jesus had to deal with competitiveness among his disciples. He had just revealed some crucial insight about Peter's future, but rather than asking pertinent follow-up questions, Peter responded with, essentially, "Yeah, yeah, but what about John?" Jesus replied, tactfully, that John's calling was none of Peter's business.

Rather than being nosy and wondering, *What about that other person?* instead we should be asking, "Lord, what instructions do you have today for *me*?"

"I really lost myself in worship this morning . . .
By the time the service ended, I was in a different pew,
a different church, and a different denomination."

57

Get Lost

[God] has made everything beautiful in its time. He has also set
eternity in the human heart.

Ecclesiastes 3:11

When used in Scripture, the word *lost* almost always has negative
connotations and is often linked to anxiety-producing circumstances.
Sometimes it refers to a valuable item that was misplaced. Or worse,
other times it applies to people who were separated from God, subject
to death were it not for a loving Savior (Luke 19:10).

Lost usually suggests a detachment of some kind. That can be a
bad thing, as when King David was lost in grief after the death of his
son Absalom. Even though Absalom's rebellion had sparked a divisive civil war, his death weighed on David so much that he couldn't
even thank the soldiers who had saved the nation—and his own life
(2 Samuel 19:1–8).

The detachment can also be positive. We can get lost in love as
Jacob did after seeing Rachel for the first time. He gladly worked seven
years for the privilege of marrying her, "but they seemed like only a
few days to him because of his love for her" (Genesis 29:20).

How long has it been since you became so lost in your love for God
that you never even checked your phone or watch during the worship service or your quiet time? The most rewarding way to be lost is
by completely separating ourselves from the ever-present worries of
the world to focus on God. We will have eternity to lose ourselves in
wonder and gratitude for who God is and what he has done. But that
doesn't mean we can't start today.

"I'd ask the pastor to be sure . . . but, no . . .
I don't think you can be totally committed from time to time."

58

Continuous Attention to God ... Partially

May I wholeheartedly follow your decrees, that I may not be put to shame.

Psalm 119:80

Writer Linda Stone notes, "Attention is the most powerful tool of the human spirit. We can enhance or augment our attention with practices like meditation . . . and exercise, diffuse it with technologies . . . or alter it with pharmaceuticals. In the end, though, we are fully responsible for how we choose to use this extraordinary resource."[1]

After spending several years at Apple and later at Microsoft, in 1998 Stone coined the term *continuous partial attention*. Not to be confused with multitasking, she described this human tendency as paying partial attention *continuously* in an effort not to miss anything. Short bouts of continuous partial attention might appear to be beneficial, yet "in large doses, it contributes to a stressful lifestyle, to operating in crisis management mode, and to a compromised ability to reflect, to make decisions, and to think creatively."[2]

How often do we keep one ear tuned to what the Spirit might be trying to tell us while simultaneously absorbing input from other sources? How often do we pray or read Scripture without making mental to-do lists for what we need to do when we're finished?

Continuous partial attention creates stress and anxiety. What removes it? Attentive devotion to God. The peace of mind only he can provide will go far in making our lives more manageable—*if* we give him our full attention. He deserves nothing less.

"Until we determine if this church is a safe place to be real,
you're an international spy and I recently won the Pulitzer."

59

Pride You Can Be Proud Of

Do nothing out of selfish ambition or vain conceit.
Philippians 2:3

Pride. It's one of the seven deadly sins and, some say, the root of all the others. It's also the trickiest.

We *know* lust is wrong—and sloth, gluttony, envy, wrath, and greed. Yet we teach our kids to hold their heads up, look people in the eye, and be proud of who they are. They're told to take pride in their accomplishments. At what point does healthy self-awareness and self-esteem cross the line to become a deadly sin?

When we start taking credit for our gifts, skills, and personalities, we've crossed the line. That's why pride is so tricky: it's easy to lose sight of who is responsible for what we've done. God reminds us, through Jeremiah, "Let the one who boasts boast about this: that they have the understanding to know me, that I am the LORD, who exercises kindness, justice and righteousness on earth" (Jeremiah 9:24; see also 1 Corinthians 1:26–31; Galatians 6:14).

Is your pride appropriate? Or is it deadly? One way to know for sure is to check regularly to see who's sitting on the throne in your life—setting the direction and receiving the credit. You may discover it's time to give up your seat.

"Ruth and I would like to thank the church members who anonymously mowed our law, our roses, and our petunias while we were on vacation."

Genuine Service

Whatever you do, whether in word or deed, do it all in the name
of the Lord Jesus, giving thanks to God the Father through him.

Colossians 3:17

Most believers have a genuine desire to serve others, just as most
students have a desire to make As. Yet those students may cut short
their homework time to pursue less rewarding opportunities. Consequently, they receive lower grades than expected and sometimes the
teacher's observation, "You can do better."

Similarly, we may forget it is God whom we serve; he rewards our
service. If we approach service as a chore or obligation, people notice.
We might agree to serve food to homeless people in an inner-city
church kitchen, but do we linger afterward to help wash the dishes
and sweep the floor and maybe even strike up a conversation with
some of the people? We might be persuaded to teach a youth class,
but are we satisfied to stumble through the curriculum provided? Or
do we prepare to share our personal pains and triumphs with young
people who may be facing the future with more than a little concern?

All servants of Christ want to hear him say, "Well done, good and
faithful servant" (Matthew 25:21). Genuine service goes the extra mile.
It turns the other cheek. It emulates what Jesus would do in that situation. If we are serving primarily to feel better about ourselves or to
look good for others, those acts of kindness will still be beneficial.

But we can do better.

When the first visitor in three years entered the sanctuary,
the church experienced a major turnaround.

61

Your Hospitality

You welcomed me as if I were an angel of God, as if I were
Christ Jesus himself.

Galatians 4:14

Some of the most serious sins of the modern church don't seem to
be covered by the seven "deadly" ones. While we'll always struggle
with pride, greed, lust, envy, gluttony, wrath, and sloth, the sin of poor
hospitality is equally threatening and potentially destructive to many
homes and congregations.

People regularly come into our lives and churches looking for
friendship or hope. Often their attempt at a personal connection is
thwarted as we walk past without noticing them. Some churches allow
visitors to leave without an introduction, an invitation to return, or
even a smile. Some go to the other extreme and put newcomers on
the spot: "New family on left side, fifth pew. Swarm, swarm, swarm!"

Showing hospitality is more important than we may think. While it's
easy to become absorbed with our inner circle of friends and personal
problems, we need to be more aware of others whom Jesus may have
placed in our paths for a reason.

What if we greeted those people the way the Galatian church
greeted Paul: as if they were Jesus himself? We might be entertaining
"angels without knowing it" (Hebrews 13:2)! Jesus even equates our
hospitality to others with our treatment of him (Matthew 25:31–46).

While we may never hear thanks from the strangers we encounter,
we can anticipate Jesus's commendation for our hospitality.

62

Biblical Illiteracy

For the word of God is alive and active. Sharper than any double-edged sword, it penetrates even to dividing soul and spirit, joints and marrow; it judges the thoughts and attitudes of the heart.

Hebrews 4:12

A research study recently found that only 45 percent of those who regularly attend church read the Bible more than once a week. Almost 20 percent said they *never* read the Bible. And the rest read "occasionally," perhaps once or twice a month.[1]

Christians correctly refer to the Bible as "the Word of God," and we claim it as a foundation for what we believe. But does that matter if we don't actually know what it says? Would you trust a judge who didn't know the Constitution or a doctor who didn't understand human anatomy? Why should the secular world trust or respect so-called believers who have little knowledge of Scripture and even less desire to learn?

When the apostle Paul wrote his second letter to Timothy, he was imprisoned and expecting to die soon (2 Timothy 4:6–7). Among his final written words was a clear declaration of the unparalleled significance of Scripture. He reminded us that Scripture not only teaches and trains the reader but also rebukes false doctrines and corrects naive thinking about critical spiritual matters. Why? So God's servants will be fully equipped for all good work (2 Timothy 3:17).

Knowing the Bible can keep us from being deceived and looking foolish. Any excuse to avoid biblical literacy is a conscious choice to remain ignorant and spiritually immature.

"I was convicted by today's sermon to repair our relationship . . .
Let's start with your apology."

63

Sorry Seems to Be the Hardest Word

A brother wronged is more unyielding than a fortified city; disputes are like the barred gates of a citadel.

Proverbs 18:19

Conflict. You can't avoid it unless perhaps you live your life in solitary confinement, which is not how God wants us to live. Many scriptural teachings challenge us to get along with those outside our own belief system. We must submit to government leaders, regardless of their political persuasion (1 Peter 2:13–15). When accosted, we are to turn the other cheek rather than retaliate (Matthew 5:39).

Perhaps the most difficult conflicts are those with people close to us. If you spend much time with the same people in classrooms, workplaces, military barracks, homes, or even church sanctuaries, you're bound to have flare-ups with some of them from time to time. If left unresolved, those conflicts can escalate into physical fights, divorces, prodigal children, church splits, lawsuits, and other serious problems. Such situations make believers—and Christ—look bad to nonbelieving onlookers.

The apostle Paul provided a simple plan for minimizing such consequences: "Why not rather be wronged? Why not rather be cheated?" (1 Corinthians 6:7). It's a simple solution, yes, but not an easy one. Most of us find it easier to turn the other cheek when slapped than to let someone cheat us or treat us unfairly and then "get away with it." But if we remember who we are in Christ, he can lift us above the fray of everyday conflicts and soothe the sting of gross injustice. After all, he knows exactly how it feels.

"Pssssst . . . When they pass the plate . . . pretend you're an e-giver."

64

Spotlight on Giving

When you give to the needy, do not let your left hand know what your right hand is doing, so that your giving may be in secret.

Matthew 6:3–4

Scripture is filled with instructions and insights on money, wealth, giving to others, giving to God, and related topics. The Bible details the significance and the proper—and improper—motivations for giving. Jesus had some particularly harsh words for those who made an ostentatious show of giving to others (Matthew 6:1–4). Yet amid all Scripture's instructions concerning giving, one story seems to sum up everything else.

Jesus was sitting in the temple across from thirteen large trumpet-shaped collection receptacles where people placed their monetary offerings. Perhaps the size of the gift could be estimated audibly by the clanging racket of the coins against the sides of the collection box. A poor widow came along and tossed in two small copper coins that made little if any sound. Yet Jesus immediately summoned his nearby disciples and told them, "Truly I tell you, this poor widow has put more into the treasury than all the others" (Mark 12:43). She gave all she had, which proportionally was a greater gift than anyone else's.

It doesn't appear Jesus even spoke to the widow, yet her demonstration of a "cheerful giver" (2 Corinthians 9:7) was recorded in Scripture for all time. She didn't sound trumpets or shine a spotlight to highlight her sacrificial gift. But Jesus did. He saw both her gift and her heart, just as he sees ours.

"My new goal is to have a daily quiet time at least twice a week."

65

Make Time

Very early in the morning, while it was still dark, Jesus got up, left the house and went off to a solitary place, where he prayed.

Mark 1:35

You can't be involved in a church for long without being challenged to spend time alone with God. Few of us would say it's not a good idea, yet some people seem to have a lot more hours in their weeks than others. Most of us are busy, whether we're starting life as newlyweds, raising children, involved in various worthwhile community organizations, or dealing with constant demands from school or work. Segments of time set apart for God are often sporadic if not completely nonexistent.

Besides, we go to church when we can. Doesn't that count for something? And some of us have additional church commitments throughout the week—such as teaching, visiting homebound friends, or meeting with small groups. With everything else going on, isn't that enough?

No one was busier than Jesus. Crowds of people constantly surrounded him. If he wasn't teaching, he was healing sick people, comforting discouraged people, encouraging others, or training his disciples. He didn't get personal time or a two-week vacation each year. Yet he repeatedly sought out solitude and time to spend with his Father (Mark 1:35; 3:7; 6:45–46; 9:2–8). If Jesus needed that regular connection, how much more do we?

The time we spend *for* God should be driven by the time we spend *with* God. Otherwise, all our good deeds are just busywork.

It took twelve years to go from atheist to agnostic . . .
Another six to become a believer . . . five months to choose a church . . .
Ted's pew selection could take a while.

66

Don't Let Your Conscience Be Your Only Guide

> Be careful . . . that the exercise of your rights does not become a stumbling block to the weak.
>
> 1 Corinthians 8:9

Choosing to place one's faith in Christ is the most important decision anyone will ever make. Yet that choice initiates a multitude of questions. Which of my habits and behaviors need to be changed as I submit to Christ's lordship? What does he expect of me now? Do I need to let go of any old beliefs now that I am free in Christ?

Some questions are crucial. For example, Scripture warns repeatedly of the necessity of discerning truth, so which of the differing "truths" about God do you believe? Other decisions are more a matter of personal preference, such as which church and worship style (and pew) helps you hear God most clearly.

Some choices will be potentially divisive. In certain matters—such as Bible translations, baptismal practices, music forms, and the use of spiritual gifts—some people feel the freedom to choose from a variety of options while others insist only one option is acceptable. In such cases, we are to let God's Spirit guide our consciences.

But that's not the end of it. Even if *your* conscience is clear about your beliefs and practices, your freedom in Christ can be distressing to other believers who haven't come to the same conclusion (1 Corinthians 8:9–13). If that's the case, you have yet another choice to make.

Do you flaunt your freedom? Or do you do what is best for fellow believers? This should be one of the easiest decisions you ever make.

"Wait a minute! . . . I distinctly remember ignoring
this same sermon two years ago!"

67

Limited Time Offer! Act Now!

I tell you, now is the time of God's favor, now is the day of salvation.

2 Corinthians 6:2

"I'll get around to it someday." Have you heard that lately? Have you *said* it?

Most of us have a number of uncompleted or yet-to-be-started projects around the house, stacks of unread books and magazines, and items on to-do lists that have been postponed for months. Our intentions are good, yet new opportunities pile up faster than we can address the old ones.

Once the procrastination habit is established, however, it can quickly become a mindset. The things we delay may not be of much concern except when we postpone our spiritual commitments. We anticipate the return of Jesus someday (John 14:1–3), but if that "someday" comes sooner than expected, what will we have to say for ourselves?

The author of Hebrews placed an emphasis on "today." He first quoted the psalmist who wrote about the Israelites in the wilderness who heard God's clear instructions yet refused to act on them. Eventually their apathy and grumbling evolved into disobedience and rebellion, and they missed out on the promised land. He then begged his readers, "Encourage one another daily, as long as it is called 'Today,' so that none of you may be hardened by sin's deceitfulness" (Hebrews 3:13).

We've grown accustomed to ignoring the ongoing media blitz of "limited time offers." This is an offer, however, we dare not postpone. "Someday" is bearing down on us. Act today.

"Bad news . . . The Christian buzz word we've
been using was obsolete two years ago."

68

Neither New nor Improved

Jesus Christ is the same yesterday and today and forever.
Hebrews 13:8

Do you remember New Coke? In 1985 the Coca-Cola Company decided to alter its long-standing and widely beloved formula. Pepsi's share of the cola market had been rising, and Coca-Cola decided not to add a new product but rather to change their tried-and-true cola taste with the slogan "The Best Just Got Better!"

To many, this epitomized a disastrous product launch. Public response was overwhelmingly negative. The original product was quickly reintroduced as Coca-Cola Classic, despite public references to "Old Coke," and New Coke eventually became Coke II before phasing out altogether.

"New and improved" has become a ubiquitous claim to attract customer attention, with "old" being considered stale or outdated. And as the church seeks to reach people with its message of God's renewal, we may think newer is better. What we need to understand, however, is that we serve an eternal and perfect God who has no needs. He can't be new or improved.

God makes us new creations (2 Corinthians 5:17). He makes all things new (Revelation 21:5). The love and compassion he offers is new to us every morning (Lamentations 3:22–23). All this is possible only because God is good; he can't get better!

God changes us, but he never changes. This old truth is, and will always be, good news.

"The biggest challenge in starting a senior adult ministry
is convincing enough people that they qualify."

69

Act Your Age

> Is not wisdom found among the aged? Does not long life bring understanding?
>
> Job 12:12

When you hear the term *old person*, what image comes to mind? Do you picture a cranky man shaking his fist and screaming at kids to keep off his lawn? Do you imagine a sweet, feeble woman sitting in a wheelchair on a nursing home porch? Do you see your face in the bathroom mirror?

When children are young, we try to teach them confidence and values. We want them to take on worthwhile challenges, to find purpose in their lives, to persevere, and to thrive. So why, as we get older, do we quit following our own advice?

The Mosaic law acknowledged the respect older people should command in their communities (Leviticus 19:32). The New Testament concurs: the involvement of elders was an emphatic teaching of Paul (1 Timothy 5:1, 17), James (James 5:14), and Peter (1 Peter 5:5). Peter's words give church elders and, hopefully, all maturing senior believers a clear late-in-life assignment: don't take pride in titles or reputation, don't focus on material wealth, watch over God's flock, and be eager to serve. Fulfilling these commands quickly turns into a full-time job!

Some older people speak of being "put out to pasture," but the truth is that far too many of us wander to the pasture on our own. Resist that temptation to stop working and start grazing. Keep running for God. Your race is not yet over.

"Computer technology has doubled my work load . . .
Now, I have to write a weekly critique
of the pastor's sermon <u>and</u> his blog!"

70

The Big Finish

Were not all ten cleansed? Where are the other nine?
Luke 17:17

Many people seem programmed to quit too soon. Offices and locker rooms are plastered with motivational posters: "The job isn't finished until the paperwork is done." "Finish what you start." "Don't do anything halfway." "Winners never quit and quitters never win."

Finishing what we start is important, especially in spiritual matters. Jesus said from the cross, "It is finished" (John 19:30). Paul wrote at the end of his life, "I have fought the good fight, I have finished the race, I have kept the faith" (2 Timothy 4:7). These men had learned that the key to finishing well is regularly acknowledging and staying connected to God along the way.

Nowhere is this lesson more evident than in the account of ten lepers who begged Jesus to heal them. He told them to present themselves to the priests, and along the way they discovered their leprosy was gone. Most of them continued on their way, just as Jesus had instructed. But one did a U-turn to thank Jesus and praise God, prompting Jesus to inquire where the others were (Luke 17:11–19).

We may think we're doing everything God expects of us. But if we're not regularly stopping to express heartfelt gratitude for all he does, we're not finished yet.

71

Joyful Noisemakers

From the lips of children and infants you, Lord, have called forth your praise.

Matthew 21:16

The sounds of nature—chirping birds, croaking bullfrogs, trees filled with cicadas, and more—can be comforting and inspiring. But suppose an infant squeals loudly in the middle of a church service—doing exactly what God designed every child to do. How do you respond?

Perhaps some of us try not to scowl by gritting our teeth and attempting to smile at the offending infant (and the parents). But we never fully conceal our irritation. Those parents get the message, *That kid doesn't belong in church.* The truth is, that kid *does* belong in church. Lots of kids belong in church today, but they, and their parents, drift away because church can sometimes come across as stuffy, boring, or judgmental.

Both Jesus's critics and his disciples tried to silence the pesky children who ran around while the adults were discussing and debating. Jesus scolded the gruff grown-ups, picked up the nearest child, and held him up as a standard in the kingdom of God (Matthew 19:13–15; 21:15–16; Mark 9:35–37).

Perhaps we should pay closer attention to the positive characteristics of those boisterous youngsters. Maybe we should begin to hear their "noise" as joyful praise to God and allow a little of their spontaneous delight to rub off on us. Perhaps if we become more like them, they won't grow up to be more like us.

When a church has a history of innovation,
each Sunday is an adventure.

72

The Choice Is Yours

Go! I am sending you out like lambs among wolves.
Luke 10:3

When you were a kid, did you ever read a Choose Your Own Adventure book? Readers (and now listeners with the appropriate electronic devices) can decide at crucial plot points how the story will continue. As it turns out, we tend to get more involved when we get to call some of the shots.

Perhaps that's why some of our spiritual lives are not as adventurous as we might like. Churches do what they can to inspire and motivate us, but if we're honest, most of us will admit that at times we are indifferent.

So why not choose your own adventure? When a nine-and-a-half-foot giant wanted to fight, David took him on (1 Samuel 17). When a whole nation bowed to an enormous gold statue, three young Hebrew guys stood tall (Daniel 3). When Jesus told Peter to meet him out on the surface of the lake, Peter stepped out on the water and started walking (Matthew 14:22–33). Now those are adventures!

Jesus sent his early followers into the surrounding areas with minimal provisions or direction. Yet they came back joyful and amazed at the power God had provided for their ministry (Luke 10:17–20). Maybe we need more of that mindset today.

Living for God can be a daily adventure—if that's what we choose.

"I've changed my worship style to fit my congregation . . .
I arrive late, continually glance at my watch,
and afterwards go to a nice restuarant to complain about my sermon."

The Company You Keep

Do not be misled: "Bad company corrupts good character."
1 Corinthians 15:33

Vance Packard's book *The Hidden Persuaders* was published in 1957 and continues to sell well after sixty years. Packard was one of the first to reveal how advertising is used to persuade potential buyers. It's not always pretty.

Scripture has much to say about persuasion as well, and it's not all pretty, either. False prophets persuaded God's people to "trust in lies" (Jeremiah 28:15; 29:31–32). Jesus's critics persuaded the crowds to release Barabbas and have Jesus executed (Matthew 27:20). Men were persuaded to give false testimony against Stephen, leading to his stoning (Acts 6:8–14).

Persuasion isn't always a verbal matter. People who notice our behavior may copy it—for good or for bad. Peter reminded his readers that nonbelievers were watching them, so the believers' righteous behavior could be very persuasive (1 Peter 2:12).

Believers can even become bad influences on one another if we get confused or make premature assumptions. The Corinthian church, which was quite a mess, was troubled when some of its members erroneously said there was no resurrection of the dead. Paul went to great lengths to clarify the truth (1 Corinthians 15).

One way or another, we are all persuaders. We know we should *avoid* a bad influence; let's also be sure we don't *become* one.

"Thanks to the youth group's experience at the wilderness camp, they now know how to survive with only a knife, a compass, and an emergency evac helicopter."

74

In Case of Emergency

You are my hiding place; you will protect me from trouble and surround me with songs of deliverance.

Psalm 32:7

Do you have faith in Christ? Do you trust God to uphold all his promises? Do you regularly affirm his trustworthiness? If so, that's good. But do you also have a back-up plan—just in case?

In addition to their professed belief in Jesus, many believers also have life and health insurance, stock portfolios, pension plans, large homes, and other just-in-case "cushions." There's nothing inherently wrong with those things, of course. But we need to ask ourselves, in the event of a catastrophe in our lives, would we instinctively turn to God or to our financial resources?

Indeed, those who don't plan ahead are described as foolish in Scripture. But ironically, Jesus's two specific examples (of a builder who went bankrupt before finishing his project and a king who went to war prematurely) are used to demonstrate that his followers ought to be willing to give up everything else to be his disciples (Luke 14:28–32).

To use a phrase often attributed to Corrie ten Boom, "You can never learn that Christ is all you need, until Christ is all you have." Too few of us ever learn this firsthand because we turn to other options first. But what Jesus taught his first disciples, he wants us to know as well—in times of crisis and helplessness, God is the only resource we'll ever need (Matthew 10).

"We're first-time visitors . . .
Do you misinterpret Scripture every Sunday,
or is this a special sermon series?"

75

Everyone's a Critic

The words of the reckless pierce like swords, but the tongue of the wise brings healing.

Proverbs 12:18

"Criticism is a study by which men grow important and formidable at very small expense" (Samuel Johnson).

"Criticism is prejudice made plausible" (H. L. Mencken).

"Critics? I love every bone in their heads" (Eugene O'Neill).

Artists, writers, actors, and other creative types grow accustomed to regularly dealing with criticism—whether deserved or undeserved. Those who work in the church—pastors, teachers, musicians, and all believers for that matter—might need to develop thicker skin when unkind comments are whispered a bit too loudly.

If you keep two things in mind, criticism shouldn't bother you as much. First, remember Jesus was hounded by critics from the first of his ministry to his final days on earth. This proves that just because you are criticized doesn't necessarily mean you are wrong. So don't let uninformed comments deter you from doing good work.

Second, remember you are not Jesus. While he needed no correction or improvement, sometimes we imperfect humans do. We would do well to consider (and even invite) constructive criticism from others—especially those who love us and know us best.

It's all too easy to sit on the sidelines or in the pews and criticize what *other* people are doing. If you receive such criticism from time to time, keep in mind that at least you are doing *something*. God will eventually reward deeds, not critical reviews, so don't stop doing what really matters.

76

The Great Debate

In [Christ] we were also chosen, having been predestined according to the plan of him who works out everything in conformity with the purpose of his will.

Ephesians 1:11

Predestination vs. free will is a debate that has raged for centuries. Does God plot out every step of our lives, or do we get a say in things? Differing opinions have generated enough heated discussions and hot air to launch fleets of balloons.

We can't resolve this conundrum in a three-minute devotion, but let's consider a couple of points. Planning ahead is usually seen as a positive thing, so can't we take comfort in a God who doesn't operate "on the fly"? He has a plan and a purpose for us that began even before we were born (Psalm 139:13; Jeremiah 1:4–5). And he is not merely our Creator; he is a loving heavenly Father who "predestined us for adoption to sonship through Jesus Christ" (Ephesians 1:5).

Yet for every Scripture that mentions or hints at predestination, we can find another that supports the importance of making a conscious choice to believe in Christ and devote ourselves to God (Joshua 24:14–15; John 7:17; James 4:4). Doesn't it make sense, though, that if God has a specific plan and purpose for each of us we would *want* to discover it and voluntarily endorse his blueprint?

God has eternity to answer our questions and clarify our thinking. In the meantime, we can waste time and energy trying to resolve an apparent contradiction. Or we can focus on the many other truths we agree on. That choice is always ours to make.

Eugene, David, and Merle relive their glory days as worship leaders.

77

Quality vs. Quantity

Do not keep babbling like pagans, for they think they will be heard because of their many words.

Matthew 6:7

Sinful human beings struggle to have a consistently meaningful, growing relationship with a perfect and unseen God. The Lord's Prayer (Matthew 6:9–13) includes a request to "give us today our daily bread," so it is somewhat repetitive by design. Beyond that, we are instructed to "pray and not give up" (Luke 18:1–8) and even to "pray continually" (1 Thessalonians 5:17).

Yet as we attempt to heed those challenges and pray more consistently, we risk falling into another problematic habit: offering God our words without much thought given to them. We recite the Lord's Prayer while thinking about a problem at work. We sing praises to God while daydreaming about an upcoming vacation. Perhaps this is why Jesus peppered his Sermon on the Mount with both pleas for sincere worship and warnings against hypocrisy or an autopilot approach to spiritual disciplines.

If our hearts and minds aren't active, our "worship" is perceived as babbling. Our "prayer" comes across as "blah, blah, blah." The challenge, then, is to find the fine line that keeps you connected with God, not scaling back your requests or neglecting your gratitude, but communicating in a fresh way each time you pray, sing, or otherwise worship. "Vain repetitions" (as the King James Bible interprets *babbling*) are a waste of God's time and yours. But a thoughtful and thankful relationship with him will always give the two of you something new to talk about.

78

The Personal Touch

When [Jesus] saw the crowds, he had compassion on them.

Matthew 9:36

Considering the limited number of first-century communication options, Jesus's ministry was quite diverse. He was such a popular teacher that he often had to find physical space to accommodate large crowds, including preaching from a boat anchored just offshore (Luke 5:1–3) and on a mountainside (Matthew 5:1). For more intensive training on a regular basis, he chose a group of twelve with whom he could interact. And when it came to his miracles—especially healings—his attention was usually more personal and private (Mark 5:37–43).

The key to Jesus's effective ministry was his compassion. When we are in a crowd, we see the pokey drivers who delay us or the person in the supermarket line who waits until their groceries are bagged before starting to look for their debit card. But when Jesus was in a crowd, he saw "sheep without a shepherd" (Matthew 9:36).

Sometimes a quick email of encouragement is sufficient. More often, however, hurting people appreciate a personal touch of ministry: a warm hug, the smell of a home-cooked meal being shared, or for many who live alone, just the sound of a friendly voice.

Electronic media can quickly and conveniently reach a lot of people. But a ministry of compassion usually requires a block of time and a real live person who cares.

"Six-thirty on a Sunday morning and the senior pastor
just asked me to preach the sermon . . .
He didn't have time to prepare."

79

Ever Ready

Always be prepared to give an answer to everyone who asks you to give the reason for the hope that you have.

1 Peter 3:15

When people list their greatest fears, glossophobia—fear of public speaking—is often at or near the top. Some people try to avoid any need to speak in public; others take courses to help them address their fears.

Those who take speech classes will discover a speech can be informative, demonstrative (instructive), persuasive, entertaining, or impromptu; not all speeches induce the same level of stress. When Scripture prompts us to talk about our faith to others, many times we might be reluctant because we fear questions we can't answer about Bible events, doctrine, Christian history, or other topics. While we aren't expected to become experts on the Bible, we must be prepared to explain why we believe.

Sometimes we think we must give a persuasive speech to convert someone on the spot, but that seldom happens. Every believer has a story of how he or she came to faith. Just share your story. It's a simple transfer of information no one can dispute.

Other times we fear being "put on the spot" to give an impromptu explanation under pressure. If that happens, God tells us not to worry; he promised to give us the right words (Matthew 10:19-20).

Prepare when you can and trust God when you can't. Either way, deal with your fears and speak up. A hurting world needs to hear the reason for the hope you have.

"According to the sign-up sheet,
Eugene's contribution to the after-church luncheon
will be a knife, a fork, and a spoon."

80

Just Let It Go

Many who are first will be last, and the last first.
Mark 10:31

"What's in it for me?"

Is this ever your response when you are asked for a favor or are challenged to make a personal sacrifice? It's a common one, and smart businesses know this. The Girl Scouts is a worthwhile organization, yet they don't simply ask for your financial support. They sell cookies, providing an incentive for the donor, and people clamor to get them each year.

We may even carry the "What's in it for me?" mindset into the church when asked to serve on a committee, participate in a youth camping trip, take part in a house-building project, or be involved in another demanding ministry.

A rich young man once approached Jesus, seeking to know how to receive eternal life. The Scripture says Jesus "loved him." Yet when Jesus told him to first sell everything he had, donate it to the poor, and *then* follow him, the guy "went away sad" (Mark 10:17–31).

Jesus assured his confused disciples that for everything we give up for God, God will provide even more in this life and the life to come. Still we hold out.

What's in it for us? We are offered salvation, forgiveness of sin, joy and peace, help in times of trouble, eternal life, and so much more. But to receive these things, first we may need to release whatever we're clinging to so tightly.

Bob decides to try cross-cultural witnessing.

81

Those People

And who is my neighbor?
Luke 10:29

Sometimes we just don't know what to make of "those people," do we? Oh, sure, we know we're supposed to love everyone, not show favoritism, and treat others as we want to be treated. Yet many of us must admit to feeling a certain degree of concern (we rarely call it prejudice) toward various groups of people.

"Those people" might be those who express themselves artistically and stand out in a crowd. Or they may be the reverse—the straight-laced, uptight customers who evidently believe those who express themselves artistically have committed a cardinal sin. "Those people" may be anyone who doesn't vote like you do, who has an accent, who isn't among the ethnic majority of the community, or who differs in any of a thousand other ways.

Jesus had a different term for "those people." He called them his "brothers and sisters." He identified so strongly with them that he said any good or bad treatment we show them is like treating him the same way (Matthew 25:31–46).

Jesus told the parable of the good Samaritan to answer a question: "Who is my neighbor?" The hero was a guy who most people in his culture would have considered one of "those people." This Samaritan ignored ethnic and spiritual barriers to minister to a hurting person. What was Jesus's conclusion? "Go and do likewise" (Luke 10:37).

Of course, that's always easier to do if we first introduce ourselves.

After four hours, Larry's list of reasons
why he didn't have time to prepare
Sunday night's small group study was truly impressive.

82

Temporal Speed Bumps

Teach us to number our days, that we may gain a heart of wisdom.

Psalm 90:12

So much has been written about time management that no one has enough time to read it all. As believers, we know the clock is ticking. The whole world needs to hear our message, so we must make the most of every opportunity (Ephesians 5:15–20; Colossians 4:2–6). The time to act is now (Romans 13:11–14).

Yet even with the urgency we might feel to get things done, God does not want us to lead a frantic, frenzied existence. He established the Sabbath at the creation of the world (Genesis 2:1–3) and emphasized its importance in the Ten Commandments (Exodus 20:8–11). God actually provided more detail for that commandment than for any of the others!

God doesn't want us to waste valuable time in worthless pursuits, yet neither does he want us to cram good works into every spare moment. A weekly Sabbath should serve as a speed bump in time, regularly slowing us down enough to keep us from speeding too fast for too long, even in our work for the kingdom.

If your work for God begins to take precedence over your relationship with him, it's time to hit the brakes, pull over, and shut down your engine for a while. The work will still be there tomorrow, and you will be able to see much more clearly then.

It's easy to spot back pew people

83

"No, Thanks. I'll Just Watch."

Do not merely listen to the word, and so deceive yourselves.
Do what it says.

James 1:22

Have you ever seen kids on a playground sitting on the sidelines and watching a rowdy game taking place? Many have a desire to be involved, yet if invited to join in the game they may decline. Pastors often see the same look among congregation members who seem content to go only so far in a spiritual commitment, but no further. The possible reasons for reluctance among the kids and the church members may be quite similar:

- "I don't know the rules." Sometimes eagerness and enthusiasm are there, but lack of knowledge is the problem. The best option is usually to get on a team and learn as you go. Mistakes along the way are quickly forgiven—on the playground, at least.
- "It's not really my thing." When it comes to games, kids have varying enthusiasm about team vs. individual competition, contact vs. no-contact options, physical vs. mental challenges, and so on. Similarly, not all churchgoers are equally passionate about the same ministry opportunities. We all need to find where we fit.
- "I'm not good enough." We can tell by watching when our skills aren't on par with others'. Yet if our interest in the game is evident, an empathetic participant usually notices and becomes a mentor or coach.

The satisfaction of watching and listening from the sidelines usually wanes quickly. When you feel the drive to become part of that joyful energy, don't hesitate to add your talents to the team and see what the world looks like from the playing field.

"According to the Youth Group,
a long term commitment
is a text message with more than nine characters."

84

Spiritual Ghosting

Commit your way to the LORD; trust in him and he will . . . make
your righteous reward shine like the dawn.

Psalm 37:5–6

Ghosting is a rather recent term for an age-old problem. Two people
form a relationship, it begins to flourish, and both parties appear to
be committed to growing closer. Then, without warning or fanfare,
one of the people stops communicating. The withdrawal is often total
and immediate. The other person is left confused, distressed, angry,
grieving, and wondering where to go from there.

The term is now expanding to other relationships. It is not uncom-
mon for young job applicants to go through an interview process, be
hired for the job, and then not show up for it—or to come for a day
or two, decide it's not to their liking, and then stop showing up with
no explanation. Ghosted!

Lack of commitment is especially grievous in spiritual contexts.
Sometimes people are faithful and committed for a long time, but
then they are suddenly gone without a trace. Fellow believers lament
their departure and scramble to replace the missing person's gifts and
ministries, but the church will survive.

God is the offended party, yet he remains committed eternally: "I
have loved you with an everlasting love; I have drawn you with unfailing
kindness" (Jeremiah 31:3). God will be there, as the father was for the
prodigal son, when we who have ghosted him eventually come to our
senses and realize the separation was our loss all along.

"No problem with the web domain name . . .
Guess no one else wanted
NoFunnyBusinessInThisChurch.com"

85

Lighten Up . . . Seriously!

Our mouths were filled with laughter, our tongues with songs of joy.

Psalm 126:2

Holiness. Righteousness. Sacrifice. Atonement. Repentance.

Scripture is replete with these and other somber words. Such weighty concepts are nothing to laugh at, right? So our personal spiritual lives often take on an air of solemnity and seriousness. And sometimes that is the appropriate tone for worship.

Certainly the recognition of our sin, contrite confession to God, acknowledgment of his holiness, and related matters should not be taken lightly. Yet as God responds to our pleas, he offers abundant forgiveness, mercy, and grace. He embraces us as prodigal children who have returned home. And his willingness to put our sinful past behind us is cause for joy and celebration.

The psalms are filled with references to joy. Particularly, the "songs of ascents" (Psalms 120–134) were sung by people going up (geographically) to Jerusalem for religious festivals. They were laughing and singing along the way—in contrast to so many driving to church in our day who appear they're headed to a funeral.

"The fear of the LORD is the beginning of knowledge" (Proverbs 1:7), yet as our relationship with God develops, we will find innumerable new reasons to celebrate. We can cast off our glum and sour expressions and bask in the joy only God can provide. So if you're happy and you know it, be sure to tell your face!

"I told the pastor you felt led to tackle
the church projects no one else wants to do . . .
You're preaching the next six Sundays."

86

It's Your Serve

No one can serve two masters. . . . You cannot serve both God and money.

Luke 16:13

Tennis coaches emphasize that the serve is one of the most crucial components of the game. Players learn net play, topspin lobs, overhead smashes, and other aspects of the game, but those are all reactive tactics—helpful when the ball is already in play. The serve is the player's one opportunity for total control: a spinning wide-angle slice to draw the opponent off the court, a powerful drive down the middle, or whatever works best. Acing the serve is the easiest way to score a point.

Serving is also an essential component of Christian living. There is a big difference, however, in the motive of the groups: tennis players want to gain an advantage, while believers seek to help others. But maintaining a proper motivation as we serve can be difficult. Jesus's word to the church in Ephesus, recorded in Revelation, was quite complimentary. He noted their good deeds, hard work, perseverance, discernment of truth, and more. But he also added, "Yet I hold this against you: You have forsaken the love you had at first" (Revelation 2:1–7).

What is your first love? When helping others, it is primarily God whom we serve (Colossians 3:23–24). If we forget that, our service can become thoughtless, mechanical, and even self-centered if we do it to feel better about ourselves.

Keep in mind whom you serve and why you serve. The ball is in your hands. What you do with it is up to you.

"We finally find our place in God's plan
and someone else is sitting there!"

87

Who Saw *That* Coming?

Who knows but that you have come to your . . . position for
such a time as this?

Esther 4:14

Some people think God's plan for their lives is like a sales projection
chart: an arrow continuing indefinitely upward and to the right. But
many of us realize, in retrospect, it's more like a crazy straw—constant
twists and turns but with a sweet reward at the end.

- Esther was just trying to survive as a decent Israelite girl in
  Persian captivity, yet God's plan placed her in the royal palace
  as queen at the precise time a bold voice was needed to prevent her people from being slaughtered.
- All David planned to do was silence a giant Philistine intimidating Israel's army, yet his victory over Goliath led to a valued
  friendship with Jonathan and his first steps toward becoming
  Israel's next king (1 Samuel 17–18).
- God sent Philip away from the evangelistic fervor of Jerusalem into the wilderness, where he ran into an Ethiopian official seeking spiritual clarity. As a result, the Gospel was carried
  into Africa (Acts 8:26–39).
- Two pilgrims returning home from Jerusalem were grieving
  the death of their Lord when they met an apparently uninformed stranger on the road. They were among the first to
  see the resurrected Jesus (Luke 24:13–35).

The many twists of God's plan have a purpose. Join this list of people
whom God positioned in a specific place at a specific time. Your story
is still being written!

"I first noticed that Pastor Tim
was watering down the truth during his
'Your Eternal Destiny—Heaven or Heck' sermon."

88

Truth Be Told . . .

> For the time will come when people will not put up with sound doctrine. Instead . . . they will turn their ears away from truth and turn aside to myths.
>
> 2 Timothy 4:3–4

Adherence to God's truth has never been easy or automatic. The Old Testament contains numerous examples of people who knew exactly what God had proclaimed, yet they ignored his truth to pursue their own interests, false gods, and worse.

You'd think we would have seen some improvement after the coming of Christ. Jesus didn't just proclaim truth like any other street preacher; he modeled what godly living should look like. After his resurrection, which opened the throne room of God to all who believe (Hebrews 4:16), he sent the Holy Spirit to perpetually comfort and guide believers. We should be doing so much better now, right?

As it turns out, Jesus knew things wouldn't change as much as we might hope. He made it clear that truth is still elusive to many: "Small is the gate and narrow the road that leads to life, and only a few find it" (Matthew 7:14).

Paul confirmed Jesus's assessment. In Paul's final letter to Timothy, he looked to a future time—perhaps the times we're living in—when people would "gather around them a great number of teachers to say what their itching ears want to hear" (2 Timothy 4:3).

Some truths may be hard to hear, yet we still need to keep our ears open. Keep your eyes peeled too—that narrow road can be hard to spot.

"We designed this small group with
the working professional in mind . . .
Every five minutes, we stop everything
and check our email."

89

Distractions and Diversions

No one who puts a hand to the plow and looks back is fit for service in the kingdom of God.

Luke 9:62

First-century believers were not bothered by smartphones, social media postings, video gaming, or the thousands of other distractions our ever-present screened devices provide. But they had homes, families, and the occasional funeral to attend. What's the connection, you might ask? All these things, and more, are excuses used to explain a lack of total commitment to Jesus.

With Jesus standing right in front of them, beckoning them to become his disciples, a series of people turned down his personal invitation. They all had reasons—quite good ones (Luke 9:57–61). Yet by not putting Jesus first, they missed out on being among the very few people privileged to commune with God in human flesh while he lived on earth.

People still profess a desire to follow Jesus, but then they encounter distractions. What do we miss when we put Jesus on hold to answer a text? Or to binge-watch another season of a favorite show? Such involvements are not necessarily bad, but neither are they best for us.

Old-time farmers who plowed with mules learned to fix their eyes on a distant spot across the field and focus on it to plow a straight row. Jesus suggested the same intensity is needed to stay focused on kingdom values.

The next time you find yourself distracted by technology or some other diversion, ask yourself, *What am I missing?* Then again, you may not want to know.

"Do you have a Bible with the verses supporting
my theological opinions printed in red?"

90

Redacting Scripture

Above all, you must understand that no prophecy of Scripture
came about by the prophet's own interpretation of things.

2 Peter 1:20

Between political rivalries, privacy issues, and espionage movies, we
hear a lot about "redacted files" these days—government documents
with so much of a page blacked out that only a few readable words
remain.

Occasionally, people approach Scripture the same way. Thomas
Jefferson physically cut out the portions of the New Testament he
found most meaningful, published those events in the chronological
order that made sense to him, and eliminated the rest. His "bible" has
drawn much criticism. As a naturalist, Jefferson's redaction of Scripture eliminated most references to supernatural events and miracles,
including Jesus's resurrection.

What Jefferson did consciously, many of us do subconsciously. We
repeatedly skip over or ignore portions of the Bible that trouble us
or we don't agree with, treating them as if they don't exist. What we
should do instead, whenever we are confused or troubled by portions
of Scripture, is to heed the words of an old man quoted by Charles
Spurgeon:

> For a long period I puzzled myself about the difficulties of Scripture,
> until at last I came to the resolution that reading the Bible was like
> eating fish. When I find a difficulty, I lay it aside and call it a bone.
> Why should I choke on the bone when there is so much nutritious
> meat for me? Someday, perhaps, I may find that even the bone may
> afford me nourishment.

May the fullness of Scripture become a feast for you. Bon appétit!

Notes

16 Needy or Just Greedy?

1. Manfred A. Max-Neef, *Human Scale Development* (New York: Apex Press, 1991), 17.

23 Future Shock Absorbers

1. Alvin Toffler, *Future Shock* (New York: Random House, 1970).

27 What's Your Number?

1. Os Guinness, *The Call: Finding and Fulfilling the Central Purpose of Your Life* (Nashville: Word, 1998), chapter 9.

58 Continuous Attention to God . . . Partially

1. Linda Stone, "Linda Stone's Thoughts on Attention and Specifically, Continuous Partial Attention," accessed May 17, 2021, https://sites.google.com/a/lindastone .net/home/.

2. Ibid.

62 Biblical Illiteracy

1. Ed Stetzer, "The Epidemic of Bible Illiteracy in Our Churches," *Christianity Today*, July 6, 2015, https://www.christianitytoday.com/edstetzer/2015/july/epidemic -of-bible-illiteracy-in-our-churches.html.

Christopher D. Hudson is the author of the *Self-Guided Tour of the Bible*, *Navigating the Bible*, *Once-A-Day at the Table Family Devotional*, *Following Jesus Daily Devotional*, and *100 Names of God Daily Devotional*, and has contributed to over 50 Bible projects. He has consulted with the Museum of the Bible and oversaw the development and launch of their initial books into the marketplace. Christopher is a graduate of Wheaton College and has been an active teacher in his church for over twenty years. He lives outside Chicago with his wife and three children.

Stan Campbell holds communication degrees from Middle Tennessee State University and Wheaton College. He is a career writer and editor with over twenty years of youth ministry experience. He has authored dozens of Bible-related books, primarily for youth and seeker markets, including the first three editions of *The Complete Idiot's Guide to the Bible*. He and his wife, Kathy, live in the Nashville area.

Also from Christopher D. Hudson and Stan Campbell

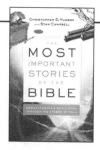

You're familiar with the exciting adventures of David and Goliath, Noah and the ark, and Daniel in the lions' den, but how do they fit together? Each one of this book's easy-to-read stories includes a brief introduction that gives historical context to help you grasp the overall narrative of the Bible and an explanation of how each story applies to your life.

The Most Important Stories of the Bible